Land of the Burnt Thigh

by

Edith Eudora Kohl

Drawings by Stephen J. Voorhies

TO
THE MEMORY OF
IDA MARY

Contents

A WORD OF EXPLANATION

I have not attempted in this book to write an autobiography. This is not my story—it is the story of the people, the present-day pioneers, who settled on that part of the public lands called the Great American Desert, and wrested a living from it at a personal cost of privation and suffering.

Today there is an infinite deal of talk about dust bowls, of prairie grass which should never have been plowed under for farming, of land which should be abandoned. Yet much of this is the land which during the crucial years of the war was the grain-producing section of the United States. Regiments of men have marched to war with drums beating and flags flying, but the regiments who marched into the desert, and faced fire and thirst, and cold and hunger, and who stayed to build up a new section of the country, a huge empire in the West, have been ignored, and their problems largely misunderstood.

The history of the homesteaders is paradoxical, beginning as it does in the spirit of a great gamble, with the government lotteries with land as the stakes, and developing in a close-knit spirit of mutual helpfulness.

My own part in so tremendous a migration of a people was naturally a slight one, but for me it has been a rewarding adventure, leading men and women onto the land, then against organized interests, and finally into the widespread use of cooperative methods. Most of that story belongs beyond the confines of the present book.

Over thousands of acres today in the West men and women are still fighting to control that last frontier, and wherever there are farmers, the methods of cooperation will spread for decades. It is a good fight. I hope I shall be in it.

E. E. K.

I. A SHACK ON THE PRAIRIE

At sunset we came up out of the draw to the crest of the ridge. Perched on the high seat of the old spring wagon, we looked into a desolate land which reached to the horizon on every side. Prairie which had lain untouched since the Creation save for buffalo and roving bands of Indians, its brown grass scorched and crackling from the sun. No trees to break the endless monotony or to provide a moment's respite from the sun.

The driver, sitting stooped over on the front seat, half asleep, straightened up and looked around, sizing up the vacant prairie.

"Well," he announced, "I reckon this might be it."

But this couldn't be it. There was nothing but space, and sun-baked plains, and the sun blazing down on our heads. My sister pulled out the filing papers, looking for the description the United States

Land Office had given her: Section 18, Range 77W—about thirty miles from Pierre, South Dakota.

"Three miles from the buffalo waller," our driver said, mumbling to himself, ignoring the official location and looking back as though measuring the distance with his eye. "Yeah, right in here— somewhere."

"But," faltered Ida Mary, "there was to be a house—"

"Thar she is!" he announced, pointing his long whip in the direction of the setting sun. "See that shack over yonder?"

Whipping up the tired team with a flick of the rawhide, he angled off across the trackless prairie. One panic-stricken look at the black, tar-papered shack, standing alone in that barren expanse, and the last spark of our dwindling enthusiasm for homesteading was snuffed out. The house, which had seemed such an extraordinary stroke of luck when we had heard of it, looked like a large but none too substantial packing-box tossed haphazardly on the prairie which crept in at its very door.

The driver stopped the team in front of the shack, threw the lines to the ground, stretched his long, lank frame over the wheel and began to unload the baggage. He pushed open the unbolted door with the grass grown up to the very sill, and set the boxes and trunk inside. Grass. Dry, yellow grass crackling under his feet.

"Here, why don't you get out?" he said sharply. "It's sundown and a long trip back to town."

Automatically we obeyed. As Ida Mary paid him the $20 fee, he stood there for a moment sizing us up. Homesteaders were all in his day's work. They came. Some stayed to prove up the land. Some didn't. We wouldn't.

"Don't 'pear to me like you gals are big enough to homestead." He took his own filled water jug from the wagon and set it down at the door, thus expressing his compassion. Then, as unconcerned as a taxi driver leaving his passengers at a city door, he drove away, leaving us alone.

Ida Mary and I fought down the impulse to run after him, implore him to take us back with him, not to leave us alone with the prairie and the night, with nothing but the packing-box for shelter. I think we were too overwhelmed by the magnitude of our disaster even to ask for help.

We stared after him until the sudden evening chill which comes with the dusk of the frontier roused us to action.

Hesitantly we stepped over the low sill of the little shack, feeling like intruders. Ida Mary, who had been so proud of finding a claim with a house already built, stared at it without a word, her round, young face shadowed by the brim of her straw hat drawn and tired.

It was a typical homestead shack, about 10×12 feet, containing only one room, and built of rough, foot-wide boards, with a small cellar window on either side of the room. Like the walls, the door was of wide boards. The whole house was covered on the outside with tar paper. It had obviously been put together with small concern for the fine points of carpentry and none whatever for appearance. It looked as though the first wind would pick it up and send it flying through the air.

It was as unprepossessing within as it was outside. In one corner a homemade bunk was fastened to the wall, with ropes criss-crossed and run through holes in the 2×4 inch pieces of lumber which formed the bed, to take the place of springs. In another corner a rusty, two-hole oil stove stood on a drygoods box; above it another box with a shelf in it for a cupboard. Two rickety, homemade chairs completed the furnishings.

We tried to tell ourselves that we were lucky; shacks were not provided for homesteaders, they had to build their own—but Ida Mary had succeeded in finding one not only ready built but furnished as well. We did not deceive ourselves or each other. We were frightened and homesick. Whatever we had pictured in our imaginations, it bore no resemblance to the tar-paper shack without creature comforts; nor had we counted on the desolation of prairie on which we were marooned.

Before darkness should shut us in, we hurriedly scrambled through our provisions for a can of kerosene. Down in the trunk was a small lamp. We got it out and filled it. And then we faced each other, speechless, each knowing the other's fear—afraid to voice it. Matches! They had not been on our list. I fumbled hastily through the old box cupboard with its few dust-covered odds and ends. Back in a corner was an old tobacco can. Something rattled lightly as I picked it up—matches!

We were too weary to light a fire. On a trunk which we used as a table, we spread a cold lunch, tried to swallow a few bites and gave it up. The empty space and the black night had swallowed us up.

"We might as well go to bed," said Ida Mary dully.

"We'll start back home in the morning," I declared, "as soon as it is daylight."

5

Oddly enough, we had never questioned the impulse which led two young city girls to go alone into unsettled land, homesteading. Our people had been pioneers, always among those who pushed back the frontier. The Ammonses had come up from Tennessee into Illinois in the early days and cleared the timberland along the Mississippi Valley some forty miles out of St. Louis. They built their houses of the hand-hewn logs and became land and stock owners. They were not sturdy pioneers, but they were tenacious.

Some of them went on into what Grandma Ammons called the Santa Fe Bottoms, a low marshy country along the river, where they became wealthy—or well-to-do, at least—by fattening droves of hogs on acorns. Generally speaking, my mother's family ran to professions, and my father's family to land. Though there was father's cousin, Jack Hunter, who had been west and when he came to visit us now and then told wild tales about the frontier to which my sister and I as little children listened wide-eyed. He wove glowing accounts of the range country where he was going to make a million dollars raising cattle. Cousin Jack always talked big.

It was from his highly colored yarns that we had learned all we knew of the West—and from the western magazines which pictured it as an exciting place where people were mostly engaged in shooting one another.

While Ida Mary and I were still very young our mother died, and after that we divided our time between our father's home—he had married again and had a second family to take care of—and the home of his sister. As a result my sister and I came to depend on ourselves and on each other more than two girls of our age usually do.

By the time we were old enough to see that things were not going well financially at home, we knew we must make our own way. Some of the girls we knew talked about "going homesteading" as a wild adventure. They boasted of friends or relatives who had gone to live on a claim as though they had gone lion-hunting in Africa or gold-hunting in Alaska. A homestead. At first thought the idea was absurd. We were both very young; both unusually slight, anything but hardy pioneers; and neither of us had the slightest knowledge of homesteading conditions, or experience extending beyond the conventional, sheltered life of the normal city girl in the first decade of the century.

We were wholly unfitted for the frontier. We had neither training nor physical stamina for roughing it. When I tried to explain to an uncle of mine that I wanted to go west, to make something of myself, he retorted that "it was a hell of a place to do it." In spite of the discussion which our decision occasioned, we made our plans, deciding to risk the hazards of a raw country alone, cutting ourselves off from the world of everyone and everything we had ever known. And with little money to provide against hardships and emergencies.

At that time the country was emerging from the era of straggling settlers. Immigration was moving west in a steady stream. The tidal wave which swept the West from 1908 to the World War was almost upon us although we could not see it then. But, we thought, there would be new people, new interests, and in the end 160 acres of land for Ida Mary. Perhaps for me the health I had sought so unsuccessfully.

Primarily a quarter-section of land was the reason for almost everyone coming west. As people in the early pioneer days had talked of settling in Nebraska and Kansas and the eastern Dakotas, they now talked about the country lying farther on—the western Dakotas, Wyoming, Montana, Colorado. Over the Midwest the homestead idea was spreading rapidly to farm and hamlet and city. One heard a great deal about families leaving their farms and going west to get cheap land; of young college men who went out to prove up a quarter-section. The land would always be worth something, and the experience, even for a short time, was a fruitful one in many ways.

To the public, however, not so romantically inclined, the homesteaders were the peasantry of America. Through the early homesteading days folk who "picked up and set themselves down to grub on a piece of land" were not of the world or important to it. But the stream of immigration to the land was widening, flowing steadily on.

How did one go about homesteading? we asked. Well, all you had to do to get a deed to a quarter-section—160 acres of land—was to file on it at the nearest Land Office, live on it eight months, pay the government $1.25 an acre—and the land was yours. Easy as falling off a log!

The only improvement required by the government was some sort of abode as proof that one had made the land his bona-fide residence for the full eight months.

What would that cost? And the whole undertaking? It depended partly on what kind of shack one built and whether he did it himself or hired it done. A shack cost all the way from $25 to $100 or more.

Some of those who had families and intended to stay, built cheap two- and three-room houses.

Of course, it cost women who had to hire things done more to homestead. But with grub, fuel and other necessities we figured it would cost not more than $500 all told.

Then we learned of this quarter-section with a shack already built, bunk and all. It had been filed on and the owner had left before proving-up time so that the claim, shack and all, had reverted to the government. We had about $300 saved up, and this was enough, we decided, to cover homesteading expenses, inasmuch as the shack was provided. So we had all but the final payment of $200 to the government, which would be due when we had "made proof."

We decided to let the money for that final payment take care of itself. The thing to do was to get hold of a piece of land before it was all gone. To hear people talk, it was the last day of grace to apply for a claim. They talked like that for ten years. We did not know there were several million acres lying out there between the Missouri and the Pacific waiting to be settled. We would have all winter to figure out how to prove up. And we found that one could get $1000 to $1500 for a raw claim after getting a deed to it.

The claim with the shack on it was in South Dakota, thirty miles from a town called Pierre. We looked that up in the geography to make sure it really existed. But when we tried to get detailed information, facts and figures to help us prepare for what was to come, we got only printed pamphlets of rules and regulations which were of no real help at all. Land Offices were so busy in those days that all they could do was to send out a package of printed information that no one could understand.

Armed with our meager array of facts, we talked to our father— as though the information we gave him so glibly had any real bearing on this precarious undertaking of his two young daughters. Whatever his doubts and hesitations, he let us decide for ourselves; it was only when we boarded the old Bald Eagle at St. Louis one summer day in 1907, bound up the river, that he clung to our hands as though unable to let us go, saying, "I'm afraid you are making a mistake. Take care of yourselves."

"It will be all right," Ida Mary told him cheerfully. "It is only for eight months. Nothing can happen in eight months."

The first emergency arose almost at once. We started up the Mississippi in high spirits, but by the time we reached Moline, Illinois, I was taken from the boat on a stretcher—the aftermath of typhoid fever. It was bad enough to be ill, it was worse to have an unexpected drain on our funds, but worst of all was the fear that someone might file on the claim ahead of us. For a week or ten days I could not travel, but Ida Mary went ahead to attend to the land-filing and the buying of supplies so that we could start for the homestead as soon as I arrived.

The trip from Moline to Pierre I made by train. Ida Mary was at the depot to meet me, and at once we took a ferry across the river to Ft. Pierre. The river was low and the ever-shifting sandbars rose up to meet the skiffs. Ft. Pierre was a typical frontier town, unkempt and unfinished, its business buildings, hotel and stores, none of more than two stories, on the wide dirt road called Main Street. At one end of Main Street flowed the old Missouri, at the other it branched off into trails that lost themselves in the prairie.

Beyond Main Street the houses of the little town were scattered, looking raw and new and uncomfortable, most of them with small, sunburned, stunted gardens. But there was nothing apologetic about Ft. Pierre. "We've done mighty well with what we've had to work with," was its attitude.

Section 18, Range 77W—about thirty miles from Pierre. It seemed more real now. The hotel proprietor promised to find us a claim locator to whom that cryptic number made sense.

The next morning at sun-up we were on our way. At that hour the little homestead town of Ft. Pierre lay quiet. Other homesteaders were ready to start out: a farmer and his wife from Wisconsin, who were busy sandwiching their four children into a wagon already filled with immigrant goods, a cow and horse tied on behind.

At a long table in the fly-specked hotel dining room we ate flap-jacks and fried potatoes and drank strong coffee in big heavy cups. Then, at long last, perched on the seat of the claim locator's high spring wagon, we jolted out of town, swerving to let a stagecoach loaded with passengers whip past us, waiting while a team of buffalo ambled past, and finally jogged along the beaten road through the bad lands outside of town.

Beyond the rough bad lands we came upon the prairie. We traveled for miles along a narrow, rutted road crossed now and then by dim trails leading nowhere, it seemed. Our own road dwindled to a rough trail, and the spring wagon lurched over it while we clung to the sides to ease the constant jolting, letting go to pull our hats over our eyes which ached with the glare, or over the back of our necks which were blistered from the sun.

Our frantic haste to arrive while the land lasted seemed absurd now. There was land enough for all who wanted it, and few enough to claim it. All that weary day we saw no people save in the distance a few homesteaders mowing strips of the short dry grass for hay. Now and then we passed a few head of horses and a cow grazing. Here and there over the hot, dusty plain we saw shacks and makeshift houses surrounded by patches of corn or flax or dried-up garden. Why were the houses so scattered, looking as though they had been thrown down at random? "They had to be set on the claims," our locator said dryly.

About noon we stopped at a deserted ranch house, surrounded by corrals—a camp, our driver explained, where some stockman held his cattle overnight in driving them to market. Here we ate a lunch and the locator fed and watered the team, refilling the jars from an old well with its long wooden water troughs.

There the trail ended. Now we struck out over a trackless land that grew rougher the farther we went. To look for a quarter-section here was like looking for a needle in a haystack. It was late summer and the sun beat down on the hot prairie grass and upon our heads. We had driven all day without sign of shade—and save for that brief interval at noon, without sight of water. Our faces and hands were blistered, our throats parched from the hot wind.

This was not the West as I had dreamed of it, not the West even of banditry and violent action. It was a desolate, forgotten land, without vegetation save for the dry, crackling grass, without visible tokens of fertility. Drab and gray and empty. Stubborn, resisting land. Heroics wouldn't count for much here. It would take slow, back-breaking labor, and time, and the action of the seasons to make the prairie bloom. People had said this was no place for two girls. It began to seem that they were right.

And this was the goal of our long journey—the tar-paper shack. We pushed the trunk over in front of the door which had no lock, piled the chairs and suitcases on top of the trunk; spread a comfort over the criss-cross rope bed and threw ourselves across it without undressing. We had no gun or other weapon for protection and were not brave enough to use one had we possessed it.

The little cellar windows which stood halfway between the low ceiling and the floor were nailed shut. But we needed neither window nor door, so far as air was concerned. It poured through the wide cracks like water through a sieve.

While we tossed, too tired and sick at heart to sleep, I asked: "What became of the young man who built this shack?"

"He lived here only a few weeks and abandoned it," Ida Mary explained. "The claim reverted to the government, shack, bunk and all. He couldn't stick it out."

———————————

The next morning we awoke to a world flooded with sunshine, and it was the surprise of our lives that we had lived to see it.

Ida started the oil stove and put on the coffee. Wearily I dragged myself out of bed. We fried bacon, made toast, unpacked our few dishes. Discovering that a hinged shelf on the wall was intended for a table, we put it up and set our breakfast on it. We found that we were really hungry.

Our determination to start back home was still unshaken, but we had reckoned without the prairies. We were marooned as on a desert island. And more pressing, even, than some way of getting back to Pierre—and home—was the need for water. We must get a jug of water somewhere. Water didn't come from a tap on the prairies. We began to wonder where it did come from; certainly there wasn't a drop to be found on Ida Mary's claim.

In the glaring morning sun which blazed on the earth, we saw a shack in the distance, the reflection of the sun on yellow boards. It was farther away than it appeared to be with the bright light against it.

This new home was larger than the regulation shack, and it had a gable—a low-pitched roof—which in itself was a symbol of permanence in contrast to the temporary huts that dotted the plains. It was made of tongue-and-groove drop-siding, which did away with the need of tar paper, and in the homestead country marked a man's prestige and solidity.

We were met at the open door by a pretty, plump young woman. A little girl of seven stood quietly at one side, and a little boy, perhaps five, at the other. As we stood there with the jug she broke into a pleasant laugh. "You've come for water! We have no well, but Huey hauled two barrels this morning from Crooks's, several miles away."

We were led into a large room, clean and cool. After one has been in a low, slant-roofed, tar-papered shack that becomes an oven when the sun shines on it, entering a house with a gable is almost like going into a refrigerator. There wasn't much in the room except beds and a sewing machine. The floor, on which a smaller child was playing, was bare except for a few rag rugs, but shining. An opening led into a small lean-to kitchen with a range in one corner; in the other a large square table spread with a checked tablecloth was set ready for the

KOHL

next meal, and covered with a mosquito bar. The home, the family, gave one a feeling of coming to anchor in a sea of grass and sky.

We learned that the name was Dunn and that they were dirt farmers from Iowa, but they had not come in time to do much farming that season. They had thrown up a makeshift barn as a temporary shelter for the horses and one cow until they could build a real barn—after they found out what the soil would do, Mrs. Dunn explained.

She hurried out to the kitchen, talking as she moved about, and came in with coffee and a plate of oatmeal cookies.

"I am so glad you are going to live here," she told us. "Neighbors within a mile and a half! I won't feel so much alone with neighbors close by to chat with."

We hadn't the courage to tell her that we weren't going to stay.

"You must have found the shack dirty," she said, with a glance at her spotless house. "A bachelor homesteader had it and they are always the worst. They wait until the floor is thick with dirt and grease and then spread newspapers over it to cover up the dirt. You'll have a time getting it fixed as you want it."

We wondered how anyone made a home of a tar-paper shack. To hear Mrs. Dunn's casual remarks, one would think it no more of a problem than redecorating a city home.

As we started on the trek back, she called after us, "Huey will haul you over a keg of water tomorrow."

As soon as we were out of earshot I said, "We can hire Mr. Dunn to take us back to Pierre."

"That's an idea," Ida Mary agreed.

By the time we had walked back the mile and a half—which seemed five in the scorching heat—it was past noon and we were completely exhausted. So we did not get started back to Pierre that day. But we felt a little easier. There was a way to get out.

12

II. DOWN TO GRASS ROOTS

There is a lot of sound common sense in the saying about leaving the cage door open. As long as we knew we could be taken back to town we were content to stay for a day or two, and take a look at the country while we were there—by which we meant that we would gaze out over the empty spaces with a little more interest.

We strained our eyes for sight of moving objects, for signs of life. Once we saw a team and wagon moving toward the south. As suddenly as it had appeared it dropped out of sight into a ravine. A horseman crossing the plains faded into the horizon.

As our vision gradually adjusted itself to distance we saw other homestead abodes. The eye "picked up" these little shacks across the plains, one by one.

For years straggling settlers had moved on and off the prairie—and those who stayed barely made a mark on the engulfing spaces. The unyielding, harsh life had routed the majority of homesteaders—they had shut the door behind them and left the land to its own.

All over the plains empty shacks told the tale. They stood there with the grass grown up around them, the unwritten inscription: "This quarter-section has been taken." Dilapidated; the tiny window or two boarded up; boards cracked or fallen apart. They, too, had not been able to weather the hard forces of nature on the frontier. If the shack had gone down, or had been moved in the night by some more ambitious homesteader, there was always the pile of tin cans to mark the spot. They stayed and rusted.

And from the tin cans ye knew them. Bachelors' huts were always surrounded; where there was a woman to do the cooking there were fewer cans. But as a rule the shack dwellers lived out of tin cans like city apartment dwellers.

But for the most part the land was inhabited by coyotes and prairie dogs, with a few herds of range sheep and cattle. Few of the homesteaders were permanent. They stayed their eight months—if they could stick it out—and left at once. Their uneasy stay on the land was like the brief pause of migratory birds or the haphazard drifting of tumble weeds that go rolling across the plains before the wind, landing against a barbed-wire fence or any other object that blocked their way.

The empty shacks reminded one of the phantom towns which men had thrown up breathlessly and abandoned when the search for gold had proved illusory. Only permanency could dig the gold of fertility from the prairie, and thus far the people who had made a brief attempt to cope with it had been in too much of a hurry. Those abandoned quarter-sections had defeated the men who would have taken them.

The main movement over the plains was that of hauling water from the few wells in the country, or from one of two narrow creeks that twisted through the parched land and vanished into dry gulches. They were now as dry as a bone.

"I'd have a well," Huey Dunn said, "if I could stop hauling water long enough to dig one." That was the situation of most of the homesteaders.

Most of these migratory homesteaders wanted the land as an investment—to own it and sell it to some eastern farmer or to a rancher. Some, like Huey Dunn, came to make a permanent home and till the land. These few dirt farmers raised patches of corn, and while the farmers from Iowa and Illinois were scornful of the miniature stalks, the flavor of the sweet corn grown on the dry sod was unsurpassed. The few patches of potatoes were sweet and mealy. But the perfect sod crop was flax. Already the frontier was becoming known for its flax raising.

We saw no large range herds, though there were no herd laws to keep them off private property. One could drive straight as the crow flies from Pierre to Presho, forty or fifty miles, without stopping to open a gate. If one struck a fence around a quarter-section here or there he either got out and cut the wire in two, or drove around the corner of the fence, depending upon how he felt about fences being in the way.

No wonder sheep-herders went crazy, we thought, swallowed up by that sea of brown, dry grass, by the endless monotony of space.

I think what struck us most those first days was the realization that the era of pioneers had not ended with covered wagon days; that there were men and women, thousands of them, in our own times, living under pioneer conditions, fighting the same hardships, the same obstacles, the same primitive surroundings which had beset that earlier generation.

Toward evening, that first day, sitting on the little board platform in front of the door where there was a hint of shade and a suggestion of coolness in the air, we saw two animals approaching.

"I never saw dogs like that, did you?" I said to Ida Mary when they came a little closer.

She jumped up, crying "Wolves!" We had seen one on the road out from Pierre. We ran into the shack, nailed the door shut that night—no risking of trunks or boxes against it—crawled into bed and lay there for hours, afraid to speak out loud.

Huey Dunn came next day with the keg of water. "Wolves?" he said, as we told him of the experience. "They wouldn't hurt anyone, unless they were cornered—or hungry."

"But how," demanded Ida Mary, "were we to tell when they were hungry?"

Huey laughed at that. When the snow lay deep on the ground for a long time after a blizzard, and there was no way to get food, they sometimes attacked sheep or cattle, and they had been known to attack persons, but not often. They generally went in packs to do their foraging.

"Goin' back tomorrow?" Mr. Dunn ejaculated, as we interrupted his talk about the country to ask him to take us to Pierre. "Why, my wife planned on your comin' over to dinner tomorrow." But if we wanted to go the next day—sure, he could take us. Oh, he wouldn't charge us much. As he drove away he called back, "Don't get scared when you hear the coyotes. You'll get used to 'em if you stay."

And that night they howled. We were awakened by the eerie, hair-raising cry that traveled so far over the open prairie and seemed so near; a wild, desolate cry with an uncannily human quality. That mournful sound is as much a part of the prairie as is the wind which blows, unchecked, over the vast stretches, the dreary, inescapable voice of the plains. The first time we heard the coyotes there seemed to be a hundred of them, though there were probably half a dozen. All Huey Dunn's assurance that they were harmless and that it was a nightly occurrence failed to calm us.

When Huey got home his wife asked what he thought of their new neighbors.

"Right nice girls to talk to," Huey said, "but damn poor home-steaders. Beats the devil the kind of people that are taking up land. Can't develop a country with landowners like that. Those girls want to go home. Already. I said you wanted 'em to come over to dinner to-morrow noon. Maybe you can fix up something kinda special."

"I'll drop a few extra spuds into the pot and bake a pan of corn-bread—they'll eat it," Mrs. Dunn predicted cheerfully. She was right.

Bringing us back to the claim the next afternoon Huey suddenly remembered that he had promised a neighbor to help string barb-wire the following day. But—sure—he could take us to town 'most any day after that.

The next day we began to discover the women who were living on homesteads and who, in their own way, played so vital a part in developing the West. One of our nearest neighbors—by straining our eyes we could see her little shack perched up against the horizon—put on her starched calico dress and gingham apron and came right over to call. The Widow Fergus, she said she was.

She sat down, laid her big straw hat on the floor beside her (no, just let it lie there—she always threw it off like that) and made herself comfortable. Her graying hair, parted in the middle and done up in a knot in the back, was freshly and sleekly combed. She was brown as a berry and just the type of hard-working woman to make a good home-steader, with calloused, capable, tireless hands. She was round, bustling and kind. The Widow Fergus had taken up a homestead with her young son.

She looked at the unopened baggage, the dirty shack. Now that was sensible, she said, to rest a few days—it was so nice and quiet out here. Homesick? My, no. There was no time to get homesick. Too much to do getting by on a homestead. Women like the Widow Fergus, we were to discover, had no time for self-pity or lamenting their rigorous, hard lives. They did not, indeed, think in terms of self-pity. And they managed, on the whole, to live rich, satisfying lives and at the same time to prepare the way for easier, pleasanter lives for the women who were to follow them.

When she left she said, "Now, come over, girls, and anything you want, let me know...."

A little later that same day we saw three riders galloping across the plains, headed straight for our shack. They stopped short, swung off their ponies, three girl homesteaders.

They rode astride, wore plain shirtwaists and divided skirts. Two of them wore cheap straw hats much like those worn by farmers in the fields everywhere. They swung from their saddles as easily as though they wore breeches and boots.

"How did you learn we were here?" I asked, curious to know how news could travel over these outlying spaces.

"Huey Dunn told it over at the road ranch while I was waiting there for the mail," the oldest of the girls explained, "so I just rode around and picked up the girls."

One would think they lived in the same city block, so nonchalant was she over the round-up, but "only eighteen miles," she explained easily.

Her name was Wilomene White, she told us, and she came from Chicago. She had been out here most of the time for almost two years—what with leaves of absence in the winter prolonging the term of residence. She was a short, plump woman whom we judged to be in her early thirties, and she had a sense of humor that was an invaluable asset in a country like that. She was an artist and head of her father's household. Her brother was a prominent surgeon in Chicago and for several years Wilomene, besides being active in club work, had been on the board of the Presbyterian Hospital there.

When her health failed from overwork and strenuous public activities, her brother ordered a complete change and plenty of pure fresh air. So with a little group of acquaintances she had come west and taken up a homestead. It was easy to understand that she had found a change—and fresh air. What surprised us was that she took such delight in the country and the pioneer life about her that she no longer wanted to return to her full life in Chicago.

The three girls stayed on and on, talking. Girl homesteaders had no reason for going home. Days and nights, days of the week and month were all the same to them. There were so few places to go, and the distance was so great that it was a custom to stay long enough to make a visit worth while. The moon would come up about ten that night—so nothing mattered. Afraid to ride home in the middle of the night? What was there to fear out here?

Ida Mary and I still hesitated about going far from the shack. The prairie about us was so unsettled, so lacking in trees that there were practically no landmarks for the unaccustomed eye to follow. We became confused as to direction and distance. "Three miles from the buffalo waller," our locator had said. "No trouble to locate your claim." But if we got far enough away from it we couldn't even find the buffalo waller.

Even against our will the bigness and the peace of the open spaces were bound to soak in. Despite the isolation, the hardships and the awful crudeness, we could not but respond to air that was like old wine—as sparkling in the early morning, as mellow in the soft nights. Never were moon and stars so gloriously bright. It was the thinness of the atmosphere that made them appear so near the earth, we were told.

While the middle of the day was often so hot we panted for breath, mornings and evenings were always gloriously cool and invigorating, and we slept. With the two comforters spread on the crisscross rope bed, we fell asleep and woke ravenously hungry each morning.

That first letter home was a difficult task, and we found it safer to stick to facts—the trip had been pleasant, Ida Mary had filed on the claim. But to prepare for our arrival at home, we added, "There is nothing to worry about. If we think it is best, we will come home." This was eventually sent off after we had discussed what we had better tell our father, and crossed out the sentences that might worry him. "Don't waste so much paper," Ida Mary warned me. "It is thirty miles to another writing tablet."

We were eating supper one evening when four or five coyotes slipped up out of the draw and came close to the shack. Almost one in color with the yellow grass, they stood poised, alert, ready to run at the slightest sound. Graceful little animals, their pointed noses turned upward. A great deal like a collie dog. We did not make a move, but they

18

seemed to sense life in the once deserted cabin, and like a phantom they faded into the night.

Huey Dunn was one of those homesteaders who believed the world (the frontier at least) was not made in a day. He was slow getting around to things. He never did get around to taking Ida Mary and me back to Pierre. And to our dismay a homesteader drove up one day with the big box of household goods we had shipped out. The stage express had brought it out from Pierre to McClure, and it had been hauled the rest of the way by the first homesteader coming our way. Altogether it cost twenty dollars to get that box, and there wasn't ten dollars' worth of stuff in it.

Ida Mary and I had collected the odds and ends it contained from second-hand stores in St. Louis, selecting every article after eager discussion of its future use, picturing its place in our western cabin. We hadn't known about the tar-paper shack then. Its arrival stressed our general disillusionment.

We had now seen the inside of a few shacks over the prairie. The attempts the women had made to convert them into homes were pitiful, although some of them had really accomplished wonders with practically nothing. It is pretty hard to crush the average woman's home-making instinct. The very grimness of the prairie increased their determination to raise a bulwark against it.

Up to now we had been uneasy guests in the shack, ready for flight whenever Huey Dunn got around to taking us back to Pierre. But trying to dig out a few things now and then from grips and trunks without unpacking from top to bottom is an unsatisfactory procedure. So we unpacked.

Then we had to find a place for our things and thought we might as well try to make the cabin more comfortable at the same time, even if we weren't staying. We looked about us. There wasn't much to work with. In the walls of our shack the boards ran up and down with a 2 × 4 scantling midway between floor and ceiling running all the way around the room. This piece of lumber served two purposes. It held the shack together and served as a catch-all for everything from toilet articles to hammer and nails. The room had been lined with patches of building paper, some red, some blue, and finished out with old newspapers.

The patchwork lining had become torn in long cracks where the boards of the shack were split, and through the holes the dry wind drove dust and sand. The shack would have to be relined, for there was not sufficient protection from the weather and we would freeze in the first cold spell.

This regulation shack lining was a great factor in the West's settlement. We should all have frozen to death without it. It came in rolls and was hauled out over the plains like ammunition to an army, and paper factories boomed. There were two kinds—red and blue—and the color indicated the grade. The red was a thinner, inferior quality and cost about three dollars a roll, while the heavy blue cost six. Blue paper on the walls was as much a sign of class on the frontier as blue blood in Boston. We lined our shack with red.

The floor was full of knotholes, and the boards had shrunk, leaving wide cracks between. The bachelor homesteader had left it black with grease. When Huey hauled us an extra keg of water we proceeded to take off at least a few layers.

We were filling the cracks with putty when a bachelor homesteader stopped by and watched the operation in disgust.

"Where you goin' to run your scrub-water," he wanted to know, "with the cracks and knotholes stopped up?"

In the twenty-dollar box was a 6 × 9-foot faded Brussels rug, with a couple of rolls of cheap wallpaper. From a homesteader who was proving up and leaving we bought an old wire cot. With cretonnes we made pillows, stuffed with prairie grass; hung bright curtains at the little windows, which opened by sliding back between strips of wood. In the big wooden box we had also packed a small, light willow rocker. In one corner we nailed up a few boards for a bookcase, painting it bright red. Little by little the old tar-paper shack took on a homelike air.

It is curious how much value a thing has if one has put some effort into it. We were still as disillusioned with the country as we had been the first day, we felt as out of place on a homestead as a coyote sauntering up Fifth Avenue, we felt the tar-paper shack to be the most unhomelike contraption we had ever seen; but from the moment we began to make improvements, transforming the shack, it took on an interest for us out of all proportion to the changes we were able to make. Slowly we were making friends, learning to find space restful and reassuring instead of intimidating, adapting our restless natures to a country that measured time in seasons; imperceptibly we were putting down our first roots into that stubborn soil.

At first we read and reread the letters from home, talking of it constantly and wistfully like exiles, drawn constantly toward the place we had left. Almost without our being aware of it we ceased to feel that we had left St. Louis. It was St. Louis which was receding from us, while we turned more and more toward the new country, identified ourselves with it.

Ida Mary and I woke up one day a few weeks after our arrival to find our grubstake almost gone. Back home we had figured that there were ample funds for filing fees, for transportation and food. Now we began to figure backwards, which we found was a poor way to figure. There was no money to take us back home. We had burned our bridges not only behind but in front of us.

It was the incidentals which had cut into our small reserve. The expense of my illness on the road had been heavy. The rest of the money seemed to have evaporated like water in dry air. Fixing up the shack had been an unexpected expense, and we had overlooked the cost of hauling altogether—in a country where everything had to be hauled. We had paid $25 for a stiff old Indian cayuse, the cheapest thing in horseflesh that we could find.

In order to be safe we had figured on standard prices for commodities, but we found that all of them were much higher out here. Coal, the only fuel obtainable, ran as high as $20 a ton, with the hauling and high freight. Merchants blamed the freight cost for the high price of everything from coal to a package of needles.

I laid the blame for our predicament on Huey Dunn. But Ida Mary thought it went farther back than that. It was the fault of the government! Women should not be allowed to file on land.

Regardless of where the blame lay, we were now reduced to a state of self-preservation. Had not the majority of the settlers taken this gambling chance of pulling through somehow, the West would never have been settled.

It is curious how quickly one's animal instinct of survival comes to the fore in primitive lands. If we ran out of bacon we stirred flour into a little grease, added water and a few drops of condensed milk (if we had it) and turned out a filling dish of gravy. If we ran out of coal we pulled the dried prairie grass to burn in the little two-hole monkey stove, which we had bought with the cot. Laundry stoves, some called them.

To keep the water from becoming warm as dishwater we dug a hole in the ground to set the water can in. The earth became so cool at night that anything set down in a shallow hole on the shady side of the house kept cool all day.

We learned that it took twice as long to cook beans or other vegetables in that high altitude; that one must put more flour in the cake

21

and not so much shortening or it would surely fall; that meat hung in the dry air would keep fresh indefinitely—but we had not tasted a bite of fresh meat since we came.

Our homestead not only had a cabin, but it boasted a small patch of sweet corn planted by the first filer on the land. It would make food for both man and beast—for the Ammons girls and the pinto.

It was a frontier saying that homesteading was a gamble: "Yeah, the United States Government is betting you 160 acres of land that you can't live on it eight months." Ida and I weren't betting; we were holding on, living down to the grass roots. The big problem was no longer how to get off the homestead, but how to keep soul and body together on it.

If one were in a country where he could live by foraging—"We can live on jack rabbits next winter," homesteaders would say. But Ida Mary and I would have to depend on someone to get them for us. We realized more every day how unequipped we were for plains life, lacking the sturdy health of most frontier women, both of us unusually small and slight. Back of Ida Mary's round youthful face and steady eyes, however, there were grit and stamina and cool-headed common sense. She would never stampede with the herd. And for all my fragility, I had the will to hang on.

Well, we would eat corncakes with bacon grease a while longer. (They were really good. I became an expert in making them.) And we still had some bacon left, and the corn; a little syrup in the pail would take the place of sugar. Uncle Sam hadn't won that bet yet, on the Ammons homestead, though most of the settlers thought he would.

Three or four miles from the claim was McClure, a ranch house combined with a general store and a post office. Walking there one day for groceries and our mail we passed a group of men lounging in front of the old log ranch house. "Now such as that won't ever be any good to the country," one of them said of us. "What the country needs is people with guts. There ought to be a law against women filing on government land...."

"And against all these city folks coming out here just to get a deed and then leaving the country," added another. "If they ain't going to improve the land they oughtn't to have it."

"Most of 'em take their trunks along when they go to town to prove up," put in the stage driver, "and that's the last you ever see of 'em. They've gone on the next train out."

Landgrabbers, the native westerners called the settlers, no good to the country. And there was a great deal of truth in it. We began to check up on the homesteaders of whom we knew. Probably two-thirds of them would go back home as soon as they proved up, leaving their shack at the mercy of the wind, and the prairie to wait as it had always waited for a conquering hand.

Huey Dunn and the Cooks and the Wickershams were dirt farmers, come to stay. Some of the homesteaders would come back in the summertime, putting out a little patch of garden and a few rows of corn each season. But for the most part there would be no record of these transient guests of the prairie but abandoned shacks. Those who took up claims only as an investment either sold the land for whatever price they could get for it or let it lie there to increase in value.

Some of the old-timers didn't object to this system. "When the land is all taken up, people will have to pay more for it," they explained. But on the whole they eyed with humorous intolerance the settlers who departed, leaving their claims as they had found them.

A great blessing of the plains was the absence of vermin. I do not remember having seen a rat or a weasel on the frontier at that time, and many of the natives had never seen a potato bug or chinch bug or cockroach.

But one day after a short, pelting rain, I came home and opened the door and looked at the moving, crawling walls, and could not believe my eyes. Worms—small, brown, slick worms—an inch to an inch and a half long.

The walls, the door, the ground were alive with them. They were crawling through the cracks into the shack, wriggling along the floor and walls with their tiny, hair-like legs. They infested the plains for miles around. At night one could feel them crawling over the bed.

The neighbors got together to find means of exterminating these obnoxious vermin. We burned sulfur inside and used torches of twisted prairie hay on the outside of the house, just near enough to the walls to scorch the creepers. But as one regiment burned up another came.

One day Ida Mary and I, in doing a little research work of our own—we had no biologists to consult on plagues, and no exterminators—lifted up a wide board platform in front of our shack, and ran screaming. The pests were nested thick and began to scatter rapidly in every direction, a fermenting mass.

They were not dangerous, they injured neither men nor crops, but they were harder to endure than a major disaster. One was aware of them everywhere, on the chair one sat in, on the food one ate, on one's body. They were a crawling, maddening nightmare.

A number of homesteaders were preparing to leave the country—driven out by an army of insects—when, as suddenly as they came, the worms disappeared. Where they came from, where they went, no one knew. I mention this episode as one without precedent or repetition in the history of the frontier, so far as I know.

A number of theories were advanced regarding this worm plague. Some said they had rained down in cell or germ form; others, that they had developed with the sudden moisture from some peculiar embryo in the dry soil. Finding from my own further observation that they were segregated in the damper sections where the soil had not yet dried out after the rain, I concluded they had been bred in the ground.

Our need for money had become acute, but before we were quite desperate a ray of hope appeared. There were quite a few children scattered over the neighborhood, and the homesteaders decided that there must be a school in the center of the district.

The directors found that Ida Mary had taught school a term or two back east, and teachers were scarce as hens' teeth out there, so she got the school at $25 a month. The little schoolhouse was built close to the far end of our claim, which was a mile long instead of half a mile square as it should have been.

We had just finished breakfast one morning when Huey Dunn and another homesteader drove up to the door with their teams, dragging some heavy timbers along.

Huey stood in the door, his old straw hat in hand, with that placid expression on his smooth features. A man of medium height, shoulders slightly rounded; rather gaunt in the middle where the suspenders hitched onto the overalls.

"Came to move your shack," he said in an offhand tone.

"Move it?" we demanded. "Where?"

"To the other end of the claim, over by the schoolhouse. And that's as far as I'm goin' to move you until you prove up," he added. He hadn't moved us off the land when we wanted to go. He would move us up to the line now, but not an inch over it until we had our patent.

The men stuck the timbers under the shack, hitched the horses to it, and Ida Mary and I did the housework en route. Suddenly she laughed: "If we had been trying to get Huey Dunn to move this shack he wouldn't have got to it all winter."

When they set us down on the proper location they tied the shack down by driving stakes two or three feet into the ground, then running wire cords, like clothesline, from the roof of the shack down to the stakes.

"Just luck there hasn't been much wind or this drygoods box would have been turned end over end," Huey said. "Wasn't staked at all."

It was autumn and the air was cold early in the mornings and sweet with the smell of new-mown hay. We hired a homesteader who had a mower to put up hay for us and had a frame made of poles for a small barn and stacked the hay on top around it, against the winter. Most of the settlers first covered this frame with woven wire to keep the stock from eating into the hay. We left ours open between the poles as a self-feeder through which Pinto could eat hay without any work or responsibility on our part.

Then one day Ida Mary went swinging down the trail to her school, a small, sun-bonneted child at each side. The schoolhouse was much like any country school—but smaller and more cheaply built. It had long wooden benches and a rusty stove and in fine weather a dozen or more pupils, who ranged in age from very young children to great farm boys, who towered over Ida Mary, but whom, somehow, she learned to manage effortlessly in that serene fashion of hers. In bad weather, when it was difficult to travel across the prairie, her class dwindled until, at times, she had no pupils at all.

III. "ANY FOOL CAN SET TYPE"

McClure, South Dakota (it's on the map), was the halfway point on the stage line between Pierre and Presho, three or four miles from our claim. It consisted of the Halfway House, which combined the functions of a general store, a post office, a restaurant, and a news center for the whole community, with the barns and corrals of the old McClure ranch. And set off a few rods from the house there was another building, a small crude affair that looked like a homesteader's shack. Across its rough board front was a sign painted in big black letters:

THE McCLURE PRESS

The first time I saw that sign, I laughed aloud.

"What on earth is a newspaper doing out here?" I asked Mr. Randall, the proprietor of the Halfway House.

"It's a final-proof sheet," he answered, not realizing that the brief explanation could mean little to a stranger.

These final-proof sheets, however, were becoming an important branch of the western newspaper industry, popping up over the frontier for the sole purpose of publishing the proof notices of the homesteaders. As required by the government, each settler must have published for five consecutive weeks in the paper nearest his land, his intention to make proof (secure title to the land) with the names of witnesses to attest that he had lived up to the rules and regulations prescribed by the government.

Also, according to government ruling, such newspapers were to be paid five dollars by the landholder for each final proof published, and any contestant to a settler's right to the land must pay a publication fee. Thereby a new enterprise was created—the "final-proof" newspaper.

These weeklies carried small news items with a smattering of advertising from surrounding trade centers. But they were made up mostly of "proofs" and ready-printed material supplied by the newspaper syndicates that furnished the prints; leaving one or two blank sheets, as required by the publisher for home print. The McClure *Press* had two six-column pages of home print, including the legal notices.

This paper was a proof sheet, pure and simple, run by a girl homesteader who had worked on a Minneapolis paper. Myrtle Combs was a hammer-and-tongs printer. She threw the type together, threw it onto the press and off again; slammed the print-shop door shut; mounted her old white horse, and with a gallon pail—filled with water at the trough—tied to the saddlehorn, went loping back to her claim four or five miles away. But Myrtle could be depended upon to get out the notices, which was all the owner required.

One day when I went for the mail she called to me: "Say! You want the job of running this newspaper? I'm proving up. Going home."

We needed the extra money badly. Proving-up time came in early spring. To get our deed and go home would require nearly $300, which Ida's $25 a month would not cover. Besides, I felt that I had been a heavy expense to Ida Mary because of my illness on the road, and I did not want to continue to be a burden to her. She had succeeded in finding a way to earn money and I was eager to do my own part.

27

I didn't know as much about running a newspaper as a hog knows about Sunday. It was a hard, dirty job which I was not physically equipped to handle. But I had lived on a homestead long enough to learn some fundamental things: that while a woman had more independence here than in any other part of the world, she was expected to contribute as much as a man—not in the same way, it is true, but to the same degree; that people who fought the frontier had to be prepared to meet any emergency; that the person who wasn't willing to try anything once wasn't equipped to be a settler. I'd try it, anyhow.

"Any fool can learn to set type," Myrtle said cheerfully. "Then throw it into the 'form' [the iron rectangle the size of the page in which the columns of set-up type are encased, ready to print]. If it don't stick, here's a box of matches. Whittle 'em down and just keep sticking 'em in where the type's loose until it does stick."

She locked the form by means of hammering tight together two wedge-shaped iron pieces, several sets of them between type and iron frame which were supposed to hold the type in the form like a vise; raised it carefully, and there remained on the tin-covered make-up table about a quarter of a column of the set type. She slammed the form down in place again, unlocked it with an iron thing she called the key, inserted more leads and slugs between the lines of type, jamming them closer together.

"If you need more leads or slugs between the lines," she said, "here's some condensed milk cans—just take these"—and she held up a pair of long shears—"and cut you some leads." She suited the words to action; took the mallet and smoothed the edges of the oblong she had cut. I watched her ink the roller, run it over the form on the press, put the blank paper on, give the press a few turns, and behold! the printed page.

With this somewhat limited training I proceeded to get out the paper. I knew absolutely nothing about mechanics and it was a hard job. Then a belated thought struck me. Perhaps I should ask the owner for the job, or at any rate inform him that I had taken it. From *The Press* I found the publisher's name was E. L. Senn. I learned that he owned a long string of proof sheets. A monopoly out here on the raw prairie. Folks said he was close as the bark on a tree and heartless as a Wall Street corporation.

With this encouragement I decided to ask for $10 a week. Myrtle had received only $8. Of course, I had no experience as a printer, but I explained to Mr. Senn my plans for pushing the business so that he would be able to afford that extra $2 a week. Of my experience as a typesetter I wisely said nothing.

While I waited for the owner's reply I went on getting out the paper. There was no holding up an issue of a "proof" newspaper; like the show, it must go on! The Department of the Interior running our public lands saw to that. Friday's paper might come out the following Monday or Wednesday, but it must come out. That word "consecutive" in the proof law was an awful stickler. But everyone who had hung around the print shop watching Myrtle work, took a hand helping me.

When the publisher replied to my letter he asked me about my experience as a printer and added: "I don't know whether you are worth $2 a week more than Myrtle or not, but anybody that has the nerve you exhibit in asking for it no doubt deserves it. Moreover, I like to flatter such youthful vanity."

He called it nerve, and I had thought I was as retiring as an antelope. But the main reason for his granting my demand was that he could not find anyone else to do the work on short notice. Printers were not to be picked up on every quarter-section.

I made no reply to this letter. A week later I was perched on my high stool at the nonpareil (a small six-point type) case when the stage rolled in from Presho. Into the print shop walked a well-dressed stranger, a slender, energetic man of medium height. He looked things over—including me. And so I found myself face to face with the proof-sheet king.

It did not take long to find out how little I knew about printing a newspaper. So in desperation I laid before him an ambitious plan for adding subscriptions and another page of home print filled with advertising from Pierre.

The trip alone, he reminded me, would cost all of $10, probably $15. "And besides," he added, "if you did get ads you couldn't set them up." With that final fling at my inefficiency he took the stage on to Pierre.

The average newspaperman would have sneered at these plains printing outfits, and thrown the junk out on the prairie to be buried under the snowdrifts; but not many of us were eligible to the title. The McClure *Press* consisted of a few cases of old type, a couple of "forms," an ink roller and a pot of ink; a tin slab laid on top of a rough frame for a make-up table. Completing the outfit was a hand press—that's what they called it, but it needed a ten-horsepower motor to run it; a flat press which went back and forth under a heavy iron roller that was turned with a crank like a clothes wringer. My whole outfit seemed to have come from Noah's ark.

Most of the type was nicked, having suffered from the blows of Myrtle's wooden hammer. She used the hammer when it failed to make a smooth surface in the form that would pass under the roller. Readers had to guess at about half the news I printed, and the United States Land Office developed a sort of character system of deciphering the notices which I filed every week.

But running proof notices was not merely the blacksmith job that Myrtle had made it appear. It required accuracy to the nth degree. The proofs ran something like this:

> Blanche M. Bartine of McClure, S. D., who made Homestead Entry No. 216, Serial No. 04267, for the South One-half of the NE 1/4 and North One-half of SE 1/4 of Section 9, Township 108 North, Range 78 West of the Fifth Principal Meridian, has filed notice of intention to make final computation proof to establish claim, etc., etc.

Then the names of four witnesses were added and the signature of the Land Office Register of that district.

One day a man went to town with a string of witnesses to prove up. He intended to go on to Iowa without returning to the claim. That night he walked angrily into the print shop and laid a copy of his published notice before me, together with a note from the Land Office. I had him proving up somewhere out in the Pacific Ocean, having given the wrong meridian. For that typographical error the man must wait until I republished the notice. Washington, so the man at Pierre said, was not granting deeds for claims in mid-ocean. One can't be inexact with the government's red tape.

But, on the whole, the work was not as trivial as it may appear. With every proof notice published in these obscure proof sheets 160 acres of wasteland passed into privately owned farm units—and for this gigantic public works project there was not a cent appropriated either by State or Federal government.

One day when the corn was in the milk—that season which the Indians celebrate with their famous corn dance—we saw Wilomene White streaking across the plains on old Buckskin, her knock-kneed pony. Wilomene was a familiar sight on the prairie, and the sight of her short, plump figure, jolting up and down in a stiff gallop, as though she were on a wooden horse, water keg hanging from her saddle-horn—just in case she *should* come across any water—was welcome wherever she went. "It doesn't matter whether it's illness or a civic problem or a hoedown, Wilomene is always called on," people said. And she was repaid for every hardship she went through by the fun she had telling about it, while her rich, contagious laughter rang over the whole country.

Today there was no water keg bouncing up and down behind old Buckskin. That in itself was ominous. For all his deformity and declining years, she descended on us like Paul Revere.

She galloped up, dismounted, jerked a Chicago newspaper out of the saddlebag, and pointed to a big black headline.

"Look at this. The reservation is going to be thrown open. The East is all excited. There will be thousands out here to register at the Land Office in Pierre—railroads are going to run special trains—"

"What reservation?" we wanted to know.

"The Indian reservation, just across the fence," Wilomene explained. The "fence" was merely a string of barbed wire, miles long, which marked the boundary of our territory and separated it from the Indian reservation.

I glanced at the paper announcing the great opening of the Lower Brulé by the United States Government which was to take place that fall, some hundred thousand acres of homestead land. Here we were at the very door of that Opening and had to be told about it by eastern newspapers, so completely cut off from the world we were.

"What good will that do us?" practical Ida Mary inquired.

"It will help develop this section of the country and bring up the price of our land!"

That was worth considering, but Ida Mary and I were not dealing in futures just then. We were too busy putting away winter food—corn and the chokecherries we had found along a dry creek bank; patching the tar paper on the shack. Like most of the settlers we were busier than cranberry merchants, getting ready for the long winter. But there is a great satisfaction in doing simple, fundamental things with one's hands.

That evening, however, I picked up the pamphlet on the Opening which Wilomene had left. It announced that the United States Government would open the Lower Brulé reservation to entry for homesteading on a given date. At this time any American citizen eligible as a claimholder could register "as an entry" in the Drawing for a homestead. And after the registrations were closed there would be a "drawing out" up to the number of claims on the reservation. Eligible persons were to register at the United States Land Offices most conveniently located—and designated by the General Land Office in Washington—for a quarter-section of the land.

The next day I was a stage passenger on the return trip to Pierre to get detailed information on the Lower Brulé Opening from the United States Land Office. With a new and reckless abandon I listed the expenditure and received a prompt reply from the proof magnate. "I note an unauthorized expense of $10—trip to Pierre. You are getting to be an unruly outlaw of a printer."

Then I forgot the coming Land Opening. There were days, that early fall, when McClure was lifeless and I would work all day without seeing a human being anywhere over the plains. In the drowsiness of mid-afternoons the clicking of my type falling into the stick and the pounding of the form with the mallet would echo through the broad silence.

And one day in October the stage driver rushed into the shop, shouting, "Say, Printer! She's open! Blowed wide open!"

IV. THE BIGGEST LOTTERY
IN HISTORY

It is an extraordinary fact that one of the most gigantic, and certainly the most rapid, land settlements in the history of the United States has been little known and little recognized, either for its vast scope or its far-reaching importance.

The passing of the frontier, with its profound effects upon American life, is not a part of our early history. It ended with the World War. The trek of early settlers in covered wagons, the swift and colorful growth of the cattle kingdom, the land rush at Cimarron are a part of our familiar history. But the greatest of all these expansion movements was at its height within the twentieth century with 100,000,000 acres of Public Land opened by the government for settlement, waste land which in a few seasons produced crops, supported villages, towns, and finally cities, in their lightning growth.

In a sense the United States Government conducted a vast lottery, with land as stakes, and hundreds of thousands of men and women gambling their time and strength and hope on the future of the West.

The land so lavishly disposed of was the white man's last raid on the Indian. The period of bloody warfare was long past. The last struggle against confiscation of Indian land was over, and the Indians were segregated, through treaties, on tracts designated by the government, "like the cattle on the range being driven back to winter pasture or the buffalo driven off the plains," to which they mournfully compared their fate. And if there is anything an Indian hates it is boundaries.

The migration and settlement of vast numbers of people has changed world history time and time again. And the Americans have been a migrating people. From the early years of their first settlement of the colonies there had been a steady movement toward the West. Without the West with its great Public Lands the United States as it has become could hardly have existed. While there was a frontier to develop, land for the small owner, there would always be independence.

European theories might influence the East from time to time, but there was always a means of escape for the man or woman oppressed by labor conditions, by tendencies to establish class distinctions. Public Land! On the land men must face primitive conditions as best they could, but they were independent because the land was their own, their earnings their own.

For many years the Public Land seemed inexhaustible; it was not until the Civil War had been waged for two years, with the country disrupted by conflict, and people looking—as they will in times of disaster—for a place where they might be at peace, that they realized the desirable land at the government's disposal was gone. But there remained the land of the red men, and white settlers looked on it and found it good. They raised a clamor for it, and the most determined staked out their claims and lived on it regardless of treaty.

As a result, the government yielded to public pressure and took over the land from the Indians, forcing them back once more. It wasn't quite as simple as it sounds, of course; it took some twenty-five years and nearly a thousand battles of one kind and another to do it. But at the end of that time the land again had been absorbed by the people, settled in accordance with the Homestead Act of 1862, and the demand continued.

The government then bought Oklahoma from the Indians in 1889. It was impossible to satisfy all those who wanted homesteads and difficult to choose those who should have them. A plan was therefore hit upon to give everyone a chance. On the day of the Oklahoma Opening, throngs of white settlers stood at the boundary and at a given signal rushed upon the land, taking it by speed and strategy and trickery— and too often by violence.

Within twenty-four hours the land was occupied; within a week there were frame buildings over the prairie, and villages and towns followed at a speed inconceivable to the foreign nations which looked on, breathless and staggered at the energy of a people who measured the building of a western empire not by generations but by seasons.

And the demand for land continued. There was a depression in the East and jobs were hard to get; with the growth of factories many young men and women had flocked from farms and villages to cities, and they were not finding conditions to their liking. They wanted to return to the life they knew best, the life of the farm. In the more populous sections the price of land was rising and was already beyond the reach of many pocketbooks. There remained only Public Land—land which was allotted to the Indians.

The government, accordingly, began to withdraw from the Indian Allotments great tracts, by further treaties and deals, slashing boundary lines, relegating the Indians to the unceded part of the land. The great tracts thus acquired were then surveyed into quarter-sections and thrown open to homesteading. In order to prevent the violence which had attended the Oklahoma land opening, a new method was hit upon. A proclamation was issued by President Theodore Roosevelt, announcing the opening of land on the Lower Brulé Indian Reservation.

As I had learned on that flying trip to Pierre, the operation of the plan was very simple. Land-seekers were to register at the Land Office in Pierre, making an affidavit showing their qualifications to enter, at which time each would receive a number. On a given day, October 12, 1907, the numbered envelopes containing the affidavits, which had been deposited in large containers, fastened and sealed so that they could not be opened, were to be drawn by lot, after having been thoroughly mixed—as many numbers drawn as there were quarter-sections to dispose of. The first person whose number corresponded with the number drawn had first choice of the land.

Government posters and advertisements for the land opening were published in every section of the country. And along with the government publicity appeared the advertisements of the railroads. For them increased population in this area was a crying need. While we had drowsed through the lazy autumn days, advertising campaigns were shrieking to the people all over the country of the last frontier.

And that October day "it blowed wide open!"

Into the little town of Pierre they swarmed—by train, by stage-coach, by automobile, by wagon, on foot—men and women from every part of the country, from almost every state—people who had been crowded out of cities, people who wanted to settle as real dirt farmers, people who wanted cheap land, and the inevitable trailers who were come prepared to profit by someone else's good luck.

Like a thundering herd they stampeded the United States Land Office at Pierre. "The Strip! The Strip!" one heard on every side. It was called the Strip because the tract was long and narrow. One day the little frontier town of Pierre drowsed through a hot afternoon, and the broad plains lay tenantless, devoid of any sign that men had passed that way. The next day the region swarmed with strangers.

Sturdy, ruddy-faced farmers, pale-looking city boys, young girls alert, laughing—all sons and daughters of America—not an immigrant peasant among them; plumbers and lawyers, failures and people weary of routine, young men from agricultural colleges eager to try scientific methods of farming and older men from Europe prepared to use the methods they had found good for generations; raucous land agents and quiet racketeers alert for some way of making easy money from the tense, anxious, excited throng.

For many of that jostling, bewildered, desperately anxious throng the land was their last chance to establish themselves. And yet the atmosphere was that of a local fair, loud with shouting, with barkers crying their wares, with the exclamations of wonder of people looking upon a new country. And the air was heavy with the tense excitement and suspense that attends any gambling game.

McClure, the Halfway House, where my little print shop had been thrown up, was the only stopping place in that part of the country and at the end of the main road from Pierre to the reservation, which lay some five miles on across the prairie.

All that day the landseekers pushed their way into the shed annex which served as a dining room of the Halfway House, and filled the table which stretched from end to end. If there was no room for them, they ate lunches from the store's food supply at the counter. We who had grown accustomed to the sight of empty prairie, to whom the arrival of the stage from Pierre was an event, were overwhelmed by the confusion, the avalanche of people, shouting, pushing, asking questions, moving steadily across the trackless plains toward the reservation.

Every homesteader who had a tug that would fasten over a doubletree, a wagon that could still squeak, or a flivver that had a bolt in it, went into the transportation business—hauling the seekers from Pierre or from McClure to look at the land.

A generation before people had migrated in little groups in covered wagons to find new land. Now they came by automobile and railroad in colonies, like a great tidal wave, but the spirit that drove them was still the pioneer spirit, and the conditions to be faced were essentially the same—the stubborn earth, and painful labor, drought and famine and cold, and the revolving cycle of the seasons.

"Shucks, it's simple as tying your shoe," stage driver Bill assured the excited, confused landseekers. "Jest take enough grub to last a coupla days and a bottle or two of strong whisky and git in line at the Land Office."

The settlers were almost as excited as the landseekers. For many of them it was the first opportunity they had had since their arrival to earn a cash dollar. And while the gambling fever was high it was easy to persuade the newcomers to spend what they could. Coffee, sandwiches, foods of every description were prepared in great quantities and disposed of to clamoring hordes. It seemed a pity I couldn't find some way of making some money too. I would. Without wasting time I wrote some verses on the land opening, made a drawing to accompany them, and sent it to a printer at Pierre to have postcards made of it.

Wilomene White had made some belts and hatbands of snakeskins, and she planned to put them, together with my cards, wherever we could sell them as souvenirs.

I rode in at daylight for the cards, but the town was already astir. People stood in line in front of the Land Office waiting to get in to register. Some of them had stood there all night. Some sat on the steps, cold, hungry and exhausted. But they had come a long way and could not afford to miss their chance.

Every train that came in was loaded with men and women. The little state capital became a bedlam, and the Land Office was besieged. They crawled along in a line that did not seem to move; they munched little lunches; a few fainted from exhaustion and hunger. But they never gave up.

Here at last was news that was news—for which the press of the country, and Europe, clamored. These land openings were a phenomenon in the settling of new territory, beyond the conception of foreign countries. Reporters, magazine writers, free lancers pushed in for their stories of the spectacular event.

The mere size of it, the gambling element, the surging mobs who had risked something to take part in it were material for stories. The real hero of the stories, of course, was the land itself—the last frontier. There were a few who pondered on what its passing would mean to the country as a whole.

I ordered 500 extra ready-prints by wire from the Newspaper Union and persuaded a bronco-buster to turn the old press for me.

Bronco Benny rode bucking horses during the day for the entertainment of the tenderfeet passing through and helped me at night, relating in a soft western drawl the events of the day as he worked: "Did you see that little red-headed gal—wanted one o' my spurs as a souvenir—haw haw!"

"Bronco, wait a minute," I would interrupt; "you've ruined that paper. Spread a little more ink."

"And I says, 'You shore, Miss, you don't want the pony throwed in?'" pushing the roller lazily back and forth over the inking table then across the form on the press. "She ups and takes a snapshot," he rambled on.

To my delight the postcards were selling like hot cakes at ten cents a piece. The Ammons's finances were looking up. In many homes today, throughout the country, there must exist yellowed copies of the card, the only tangible reminder of an unsuccessful gamble in the government lottery.

At midnight one night an old spring wagon rattled up to the shack and we heard the voice of a man—one of the locators who had been hauling seekers. He held out a handful of small change. "Here," he said proudly; "I sold every card. And here"—he pulled out a note and a small package. The note read:

"Your poem is very clever, but your drawing is damn poor. If I'm a Lucky Number I'll see you in the spring. In the meantime, for heaven's sake, don't try any more art. Stick to poetry." It was signed "Alexander Van Leshout," and was accompanied by a ready-to-print cut.

This newspaper cartoonist from Milwaukee was only one of many people from strange walks of life who entered that lottery. There were others whose background was equally alien to life in a homestead cabin, who came to see the West while it was still unchanged, drawn for reasons of personal adventure, or because the romantic legends of the West attracted them. People drawn by the intangibles, the freedom of great space, the touch of the wind on their faces, a return to the simple elements of living.

Standing in the dreary lines in the Land Office where some of them waited for as long as two days and nights at a time, we saw farmers, business men, self-assured boys, white-haired men and women.

A gray-haired woman in her late sixties, holding tightly to an old white-whiskered man, kept saying encouragingly: "Just hold on a little longer, Pa." And whenever we passed we heard her asking of those about her: "Where you from? We're from Blue Springs." The Land Office recorded the man as David Wagor.

It was not necessary to be a naturalized citizen in order to register, but it was necessary to have filed intention to become a citizen. One must be either single or the head of a family; wives, therefore, could not register. For that reason we were interested in a frail young woman, a mere girl, sagging under the weight of a baby on her arm, patiently waiting her turn. She was shabbily dressed, with a trace of gentility in clothes and manner. Whether she was a widow or unmarried only the Land Office knew, but it pinched the heart to realize the straits of a fragile girl who was ready to undertake the burden of a homestead alone.

"You are getting to be an outlaw printer," the proof king wrote me. "You were not authorized to incur this additional expense." But, catching the excitement of the crowds and perhaps a little of their gambling spirit, I was not upset by his reproof. I filled the paper with the news items about the Opening and sold out every copy to the landseekers passing through.

The plains never slept now. All night vehicles rattled over the hard prairies. Settlers on their way home, starting for Pierre, hurried by in the middle of the night. Art Fergus's team of scrubby broncos were so tired they didn't even balk in harness. Flivvers bumped over the rough ground, chugging like threshing machines.

The westerners (every man's son of us had become a full-fledged native overnight and swelled with pride as the tenderfeet said "You westerners") responded exuberantly to the sudden life about us. Cowboys rode in from the far ranges for one helluva time. They didn't kowtow to this "draw-land" game, but they could play draw poker. And they wasn't gamblin' for no homestead—you couldn't give 'em one. But they'd stake two or three months' wages on cards. They rode hell-for-leather down the streets, gaudy outfits glittering in the sun. With spurs clicking they swung the eastern gals at a big dance. And the dignity of the state capital be damned!

The whole prairie was in holiday mood. Ida Mary dismissed school at noon—no one cared whether school kept or not—and we put on our prettiest dresses to join the crowd. Through the throngs pushed the land locators. They stood on curbs, in front of the Land Office and the hotels, grabbing and holding onto their prospects like leeches. They had been accustomed to landing a settler once in a blue moon, driving the "prospect" over miles of plain, showing him land in various remote districts in the hope that he would find some to suit him. Now they had dozens clamoring for every quarter-section. This was their golden harvest. Nearly all the seekers were too avid for land to be particular about its location, and many of them too ignorant of the soil to know which was the best.

"Plumb locoed," Bill described the excited seekers. "The government's charging $2.50 to $4.00 an acre for that land. I drive 'em right over vacant homesteads just as good for $1.25. Think they'll look at it? No-siree!"

But we are a gambling people and the grass on the other side of the reservation fence looked a lot better.

After they registered, most of the landseekers wanted to see the land and pick out a claim—just in case they won one. The chances of winning must have seemed slim with that avalanche of people registering, and the results would not be known until the Drawing, which would be a week or more after the entry closed.

Late one afternoon a crowd stood on the border of the Strip, on the outside of the old barb-wire fence that divided it from the rest of space. And the wire gate stood open. The landseekers who had driven over the land stood looking across it, sobered. I think it occurred to them for the first time that this was a land where one had to begin at the beginning.

The buffalo and the Indian had each had his day on this land, and each had gone without leaving a trace. It was untouched. And as far as the eye could see, it stretched, golden under the rays of the setting sun. Whether the magnitude of the task ahead frightened or exhilarated them, the landseekers were all a little awed at that moment. Even I, seeing the endless sweep of that sea of golden grass, forgot for the moment the dry crackling sound of it under wheel and foot, and the awful monotony of its endlessness which could be so nerve-racking.

And by the gods, the grass was higher and thicker on the other side of the fence! "How rich the soil must be to raise grass like that," they said to each other. Groups of men and women gathered closer together as though for some unconscious protection against the emptiness. Around the fence stood vehicles of all descriptions, saddle horses, and a few ponies on which cowboys sat lazily, looking on. Even those who had come only for adventure were silenced. They felt the challenge of the land and were no longer in a mood to scoff.

Standing at that barb-wire fence was like standing at the gate of the Promised Land. And the only way in was through the casual drawing of numbers. They stood long, staring at the land which lay so golden in the sun, and which only a few could possess.

There were more real dirt farmers represented here than there had been in most of the homestead projects—men who were equipped to farm. But they were still in the minority. They picked up handfuls of the earth that the locators turned over with spades, let it sift through their fingers and pronounced it good. A rich loam, not so heavy or black as the soil back east, but better adapted, perhaps, to the climate. Aside from the farmers nobody seemed to know or care anything about the soil or precipitation. And, ironically enough, it occurred to no one to ask about the water supply.

"The land back east is too high-priced," the city laborer declared, "we can never hope to own any of it."

"We'd rather risk the hazards of a raw country," said the tenant farmer, "than be tenants always."

"We'll sell our eastern land at a high price," said the landowners, "and improve new land."

"My mother took in washing to save money," said an earnest-faced boy, "so I could make this trip. But if I win a whole quarter-section (and how big a quarter-section looked to a city dweller!) I'll make a good home for her."

A middle-aged widow from Keokuk told the group about her: "I mortgaged my cottage to come. The boys are growing up and it's their only chance to own land."

Others in the group nodded their heads. "Yes, land is solid!"

Leaning heavily on his cane a little old man with a long white mustache and sharp eyes denounced the lottery method. "'Taint right, 'taint. Don't give a feller a chanct. Look at me with my rheumatiz and I got as good a chanct as any of 'em—brains nor legs don't count in this. Now in the Oklahomy Run...." And he told about the Oklahoma Run of almost a generation before, when speed and strategy were necessary if one were to be first on the land to stake a claim. But the Oklahoma Run, for all its drama and its violence, dwindled in importance beside these Drawings with their fabulous areas and their armies of people.

Across the prairie came the sound of horses' hoofs and the heavy rumbling of a wagon. A locator with a hayrack full of seekers was coming at a reckless pace, not stopping for the trails. At the reservation gate he brought the team to a quick stop that almost threw his passengers off the wagon. Some of them were so stiff and sore they couldn't get off their cushion of hay; others were unable to stand after they got up. But the locator was not disturbed by a little thing like that. He waved his right arm, taking in at one sweep the vacant expanse to the rim of the horizon and shouted:

"Here's your land, folks. Here's your land." He was locating them en masse at $15 to $25 a head. No hunting up corner stakes. It all looked alike to these bewildered people, anyhow, drunk as they were with the intoxication that land lotteries produce.

He turned his weary team and human cargo around and started back to town. A wholesale locator had no time for sleep. He must collect another hayrackful of seekers early next morning.

Some of these landseekers tried to analyze the reasons for this great movement, the factors which had swept them along with this tidal wave of human migration. "We're concentrated too much in cities," they said, "crowded and stifled, and our roots are choked. We have to go back to the land where a man can grow himself the things he needs to live on, and where his children can grow up with the country—and have a place in it."

Our attitude toward the land is peculiar to America. The European conception of a plot of ground on which a family is rooted for generations has little meaning for people who move by the thousands onto untamed acres, transform it into plowed fields and settlements and towns, and move on endlessly to plow new fields.

This constantly renewed search for fresh pastures has kept the country vital, just as the existence of its Western Public Lands has kept it democratic. For its endurance the American spirit owes much to its frontier.

Beside me stood a thin-faced, hollow-chested young man, a newspaper reporter from Chicago. He ran lean fingers through brown, straggly hair, looking from the Strip, reaching to the horizon, to the people waiting to shape it according to their needs. "Great copy," he said lamely, but he made no entry in his notebook.

Outside another gate, five miles or so beyond the main entrance from McClure, was a little trading post, Cedar Fork, on the Smith ranch. The long buildings were said to have been a sort of fort in the Indian war days. The seekers overflowed even here, and when the swift darkness settled on the plains, stayed for the night, the women filling the store and house while the men slept in the barn loft or haystacks, or even in their vehicles.

They wrapped themselves in heavy coats or blankets against the biting chill of an October night—after a day so hot the tenderfeet sweltered and blistered under the midday sun.

The next morning there was frost, with the air sharp and fresh. The Smiths tried to feed the shivering, hungry seekers. The seekers always seemed to be hungry. Kettles and washboilers full of coffee, slabs of bacon sizzling in great pans, and, one after another, into the hot grease slid a case of eggs. Home-baked bread was sliced into a washtub. Shaking with cold, coat collars turned up, shawls and blankets wrapped about them, tired, hollow-eyed and disheveled, the seekers looked like a banished people fleeing from persecution. But they were not disheartened.

On October 14 the "Drawing" started. The registrations were put into sealed envelopes, tossed into boxes, shuffled up, and drawn out one at a time, numbered as they were drawn out—as many numbers as there were claims—with an additional number to allow for those who did not file or whose applications were rejected. Then the filing of the winners began. Most of the seekers had already selected their claims. They had six months' time in which to establish residence on the land.

The stampede was over. After three weeks of high-pitched excitement the seekers were gone, the plains regained their silence, and the settlers around McClure were left to face the frontier winter with its desolation and hardships. The void after the crowds had gone was worse than if they had never come. The weather had turned raw and gray, and there was a threat of snow in the air. Exhausted and let down, Ida Mary and I were desperately blue.

And then we saw someone coming across the plains—the only moving figure to be seen in the cold gray dusk. From the dim outline we could barely make out horse and rider, but we knew them both—Wilomene on old Buckskin. She was riding slowly as though there were nothing left out here now but time.

She wore a dark red flannel shirtwaist, a divided skirt of black wool, a suede jacket and black cap like a jockey's. There was an easy strength and self-assurance in her carriage. She crossed the firebreak and rode up over the ridge calling her cheery "Hoo-hoo-hoo!"

"She's going to stay all night," exclaimed Ida Mary, seeing the small bag dangling from the saddlehorn.

After supper we counted the dimes we had earned from the post-cards—more than $50. And far into the night we talked of the people who had invaded the Strip.

Next spring there would be life again over the plains when the "lucky numbers" came out to live on the Strip. Would the reporter from Chicago be among them, and the mystery girl with the baby in her arms, and Pa Wagor—and a young cartoonist from Milwaukee?

It was something to look forward to when the blizzards shut us off from the world.

V. NO PLACE FOR
CLINGING VINES

The settlers of the McClure district went on with their work as though there had never been a land opening. The men fed their stock and hauled fuel for winter, while the women tacked comforters and sewed and patched heavy clothing.

Ida Mary went on with her school work and I continued to wrestle with the newspaper. We put a little shed back of the shack where we could set buckets of coal and keep the water can handy. With the postcard money we bought a drum for the stovepipe, to serve as an oven. One either baked his own bread or did without it.

Huey Dunn did some late fall plowing. "What are you plowing your land for now, with winter coming?" neighbors asked.

"For oats next spring," Huey replied; "if the damn threshing machine gets around to thresh out the oatstack in time to sow 'em."

The homesteaders shook their heads. There was no figuring out when Huey Dunn would do things. This time he was far ahead of them. They did not know that fall plowing, to mellow and absorb the moisture from winter snow and spring rain, was the way to conquer the virgin soil. They had to find it out through hard experience. Fallowing, Huey called it.

Lasso said, "The range is no place for clingin' vines, 'cause there hain't nothin' to cling to." Ida Mary, under that quiet manner of hers, had always been self-reliant, and I was learning not to cling.

I lived in the print shop a great deal of the time that winter—an unusually open winter, barring a few blizzards and deep snows. I slept on a rickety cot in one corner of the room, cooking my meals on the monkey stove; and often I ate over at Randall's, who served meals for a quarter to anyone who cared to stop, the table filled with steaming dishes of well-cooked food. I liked to take the midday meal there, and meet people coming through on the stage. They furnished most of the news for the McClure *Press*.

Driving back and forth from print shop to claim on Pinto was like crossing the desert on a camel. Pinto was too lazy to trot uphill and too stiff to trot down, and as the country was rough and rolling, there was not much of the trail on which we could make any time. He could have jogged up a little, but he was too stubborn. He had lived with the Indians too long.

That old pony had a sly, artful eye and a way of shaking his head that was tricky—and try to catch him loose on the prairie with a bucket of oats as a coaxer! There were times on the trail when one could not see him moving except at close range. When he took such a spell, one of us drove while the other walked alongside, "persuading" him to keep ahead of the buggy. As there wasn't a tree or shrub in that part of the country, we were reduced to waving a hat in front of him like a cowboy taunting a bucking horse in the ring, or waving a dry cornstalk at him—but all with the same effect.

A little brown-and-white spotted animal with long brown mane and tail, he was the most noticeable as well as notorious piece of horseflesh in that region, and according to a few who "knew him when—," he had a past; a reputation as an outlaw and a dislike for the white man as a result of his part in an Indian skirmish against a band of white settlers. Now, like the Indian, he had become subdued with age and conquest; but like the Indian, too, stubborn and resentful. From him we learned much about how to deal with the Indian.

One evening when I had stopped at the school for Ida Mary we saw a snowstorm coming like a white smoke. We were only half a mile from home, but in blizzards, we had been warned, one can easily become lost within a few feet of his own door. Many plainsmen have walked all night in a circle trying to find a familiar shack or barn and perished within a few yards of shelter. Even in daytime one did not dare, in some of those blinding furies, to go from house to barn without holding on to a rope or clothesline kept stretched from one building to the other for that purpose.

We could not take a chance on Pinto's slow pace, so we got out of the buggy and ran as fast as we could, leaving him to follow. We were barely inside when the storm broke over the shack. As the snow came in blinding sheets we became anxious about the pony, but there was nothing we could do that night. We opened the door a crack and looked out. We could not see our hands before us, and the howling of the wind and beating of snow against the shack made it impossible to hear any other sound.

Cowering in that tiny shack, where thin building-paper took the place of plaster, the wind screaming across the plains, hurling the snow against that frail protection, defenseless against the elemental fury of the storm, was like drifting in a small boat at sea, tossed and buffeted by waves, each one threatening to engulf you.

Next day the blizzard broke and we found Pinto standing in the hayshed, still hitched to the buggy, quietly munching hay.

When the landseekers had left and the plains had seemed emptier and more silent than before, it had seemed to Ida Mary and me, let down from our high-pitched excitement, that there was not much incentive in doing anything. But, after all, there was no time to be bored that winter. The grim struggle to hang on demanded all our energy.

When I had first visited the McClure *Press*, I had looked distastefully at Myrtle's ink-stained hands and face, and at the black apron stiff with ink which she wore at her work. Now there were nights when, after turning the press or addressing papers still wet with ink until midnight, I fell upon the cot and slept without washing or undressing. At such times Myrtle, with her cheerful unconcern, became an exalted creature.

The next morning I would make a stab at cleaning myself up, eat breakfast on the small inking table drawn close to the fire, with a clean paper over the black surface for a tablecloth, and go to work again.

When blizzards raged they drove the snow through the shack like needles of steel. There was not a spot where I could put that cot to keep dry, so I covered my face with the blankets, which in the morning were drifted over with snow. Where did the lumber industry get hold of all the knotholes it sold the poor homesteader?

For a girl who had come to the prairie for her health, I was getting heroic treatment, wrestling all day with the heavy, old-fashioned, outworn printing press, heavy manual labor for long hours, sleeping with the snow drifting over me at night.

It was during one of these great storms that I rode in one of the last covered wagons, one of the few tangible links between the pioneers of the past and the pioneers of the present—and a poignant, graphic reminder that men and women had endured storm and discomfort and disaster for decades as we were enduring them now, and as people would continue to endure them as long as the land remained to be conquered.

One morning after the hardest snowstorm I had seen, I awoke in the print shop to find myself corralled by snowdrifts which the wind had driven up over the windows and four or five feet high in front of the door. I could barely see over the top of the upper panes.

That was Friday. Until Sunday I waited, cut off from the world—wondering about Ida Mary! If she were alone in that tar-paper shack, what chance would she have? Was she cold and frightened? With the snow piled in mountainous drifts she would be as inexorably cut off from help as though she were alone on the plains. The things that happen to the people one loves are so much worse than the ones that happen to ourselves—but the things that may happen are a nightmare. As the hours dragged on I paced up and down the print shop, partly because being hemmed in made me restless, partly to keep warm, wondering whether the neighbors would remember that Ida Mary was alone—fearing that they might think she was in McClure with me.

On Sunday, a passage was dug from the print shop so that I could get out—not a path so much as a canyon between the walls of snow, and a neighbor with a covered wagon offered to take me home—or to try to.

He drove a big, heavy draft team. The horses floundered and stuck and fell; plunged out of one drift into another. Galen got out and shoveled ahead while I drove, resting the horses after each plunge. The ravines we skirted and finally got up onto the ridge.

It was mid-afternoon when we arrived, and already the skies were closing in, gray upon the white plains. The grayish-white canvas of the wagon, and the team almost the same color blended into the drab picture, darker shadows against the gray curtain of earth and sky, until we came to the shack.

The Dunns had remembered, as they so often did, that Ida Mary was alone, and they had shoveled a path to the door for her. And she was safe, waiting tranquilly until it would be possible to return to the school again. In such weather the school remained closed, as there was no way for the children to reach it, through the deep drifts, without the risk of freezing to death.

With Ida Mary safe in the covered wagon, we started back at once to McClure. Having broken the drifts on the first trip, it was not hard going, but it was midnight when we reached the print shop.

On cold, bad days the Dunns, getting their own children home from school, would see to it that Ida Mary got back safely, and Mrs. Dunn would insist that she stay with them on such nights. "Now you go, Huey, and bring Teacher back. Tell her the trapdoor is down so the attic will be warm for her and the children to sleep." And when she came, Mrs. Dunn would say, with that clear, jolly laugh of hers, "Now, if you're expecting Imbert Miller, he can come right on over," which he did.

Imbert Miller was a young native westerner whose family had been ranchers out there for a good many years. He was a well-built, clean-cut young man who had been attracted to Ida Mary from the beginning, and whatever her own feelings for him, she liked claim life a lot better after she met him. All during that bitter winter Imbert came over every Sunday, dressed in neat blue serge and white collar. Some of the settlers said that was how they could tell when Sunday came, seeing Imbert ride by dressed up like that. He dropped in, sometimes, through the week in clean blue shirt and corduroys for an evening of cards or reading or talking.

In fact, the evenings were no longer lonely as they had been at first, nor were we always exhausted. We were young and demanded some fun, and feminine enough to find life more interesting when the young men who were homesteading began to gather at the shack in little groups. In spite of the difficulties of getting any place in the winter, and the distances which had to be traveled, the young people began to see a lot of each other; the romances which naturally developed made the winter less desolate.

Sometimes we would gather at Wilomene's for supper—honey served with flaky hot biscuits baked in one of the very few real cookstoves to be found on a homestead. Wilomene had a big shack, with blue paper on the wall and a real range instead of a monkey stove with a drum set up in the stovepipe for an oven—not many settlers could boast even a drum. And always the supper was seasoned with Wilomene's laughter.

In fair weather I printed both back and front pages of the paper, and in storms, when ink and machinery froze up—another complication in dealing with the press—I printed the front page only, with headlines that rivaled the big dailies. There was no news to warrant them, but they were space-fillers. A dance at McClure would do for a scarehead. I put in the legal notices, whatever news items I had handy or had time to set up, and stuck in boilerplate as a filler. I could not count the times I used the same plate over—but the settlers didn't mind reading it again; they had little else to do in midwinter.

One day there came an indistinct message over the telephone line, which consisted mainly of barb-wire fences, saying that the railroads were blocked by storm and the stages were delayed. I threw down my mallet and went home. There would be nothing on which to print the paper.

On the first stage to get through, four or five days later, there was a note from the proof king: "Do not fail to publish last week's paper, properly dated, along with the current issue." As long as there was one proof notice running, the newspaper could not skip a single week.

When the two editions were printed I went home very ill. During the course of a busy and eventful life I have managed—perhaps I should say happened—to be a trail-breaker many times. And always I have had a frail body which seemed bent on collapsing at the wrong time. Robust health I have always coveted, but I have come to the conclusion that it is not an essential in getting things done, and I have learned to ignore as far as possible my lack of physical endurance.

The Widow Fergus came over and waited on me all night, using her simple home remedies. It cost at least $25 to get a doctor out there, and many times the emergency was over one way or the other before he arrived. Homesteaders could not afford to call a doctor except in critical cases, and they relied for the most part upon the amateur knowledge and help of their neighbors.

From the beginning cooperation had been one of the strongest elements in western life. When no foundation for a civilized life has been laid, when every man must start at the beginning in providing himself with such basic necessities as food and shelter, when water holes are few and far between and water to sustain life must be carried many miles, men have to depend on each other. Only together could the western settlers have stood at all; alone they would have perished. In times of sickness and individual disaster, it was the community that came to the rescue. If only for self-preservation, it had to.

The next time the prints were held up by a storm I bought a roll of wrapping paper at Randall's store, cut it into strips, and got the paper out.

When I took the papers into the post office to mail, Mrs. Randall laughed out loud, but Mr. Randall said reassuringly: "That's right, Miss Ammons; learning to meet emergencies in this country is a valuable thing."

The proof-sheet king wrote: "It is regrettable that a paper like that should go into the government Land Offices—such an outlaw printer—"

I replied cheerfully, "Oh, I sent the land officials a good one. They can read every number."

And printers were not to be found on every quarter-section.

Meantime, while I was hammering the paper into shape, Ida Mary had settled the doubts of the homesteaders who feared that a slight young city girl could not handle a frontier school. She was a good teacher. She had a way of discipline with the half-grown plains boys who were larger and stronger than she, and who, but for her serene firmness, would have refused to accept her authority. Instead, they arrived early to build the fire for her in the mornings, carried the heavy pails of drinking water, and responded eagerly to her teaching. By means of the school, she began to create a new community interest.

Another and perhaps the biggest factor in the community life of that section was the Randall settlement at McClure. The Randalls threw up a crude shell of a building for a community hall and now and then gave a party or a dance for the homesteaders. Typical of the complete democracy of the plains, everyone was invited, and everyone, young and old, came. The parents put their children to bed in the lodge quarters of the Halfway House while they joined in the festivity. The older ones square-danced in the middle of the hall and we younger ones waltzed and polkaed in a long line down the outside ring.

It was not always easy to get music for both round and square dances at the same time, but Old Joe, a fiddler ever since the—Custer's battle, was it?—would strike one bar in waltz time and the next in rhythm to the "allemande left" of the square dances, and we got along beautifully. Some of the homesteaders helped out with guitars; a few cowboys, riding in from remote ranches, played accompaniments on jew's-harps; other cow punchers contributed to the music as they danced with clicking of spurs and clatter of high-heeled boots. And always the Randalls had a big kettle of coffee to serve with the box lunches the guests provided for themselves.

At Christmas Ida Mary and I were invited by the Millers for a house party. It was the first well-established home we had seen since we reached South Dakota. A small farm house, plainly furnished, but it had been a home for a long time.

The Millers were counted a little above the average westerner in their method of living. Stockmen on a small scale, they ran several hundred head of cattle. Mrs. Miller was a dignified, reserved woman who maintained shiny order in her house. "She even scalds her dishes," folks said, which by the water-hauling populace was considered unpardonable aristocracy. Imbert was the pride and mainstay of his parents. There were warm fires, clean soft beds, and a real Christmas dinner. There was corn-popping, and bob-sledding with jingling bells behind a prancing team, with Imbert and Ida Mary sitting together as Imbert drove.

Imbert's devotion to Ida was casually accepted by the prairie folk. They all knew him—a likable, steady young fellow, who seemed to have a way with the girls. Homestead girls came and went, and flirtations to break the monotony while they stayed were nothing unusual.

But when Imbert paid $10 for the teacher's box at a box-social held at the schoolhouse one night, the old-timers gaped. It looked, they said, as if that little tenderfoot teacher had Imbert Miller lariated. It beat thunder how the western fellows did fall for eastern schoolmarms. Ten dollars for a shoe box, without knowing what there was in it! Most of the bachelor homesteaders bought boxes with a view to what they would get to eat—potato salad and homemade cake.

Because we were no longer oppressed by a sense of loneliness, Ida and I came to love best of all the evenings at home in the tiny shack with its gay cushions and bright curtains; we enjoyed the good hot supper of spuds and bacon, or rabbit which some neighbor had brought; hot biscuits, chokecherry jelly and coffee simmering gently on the back of the stove. Such a feast, however, was only on rare occasions. After supper, with the world shut out, we read the mail from home. "You've done so well, girls, I'm proud of you," our father wrote. "I'll be looking to see you home next spring."

I believe Ida Mary was happier that winter than she had ever been, and her work was easier for her than mine for me, with fewer hardships, thanks to the Dunns and to Imbert who did much to make it easier for her.

During that whole winter the Randalls were the mainstay of the community. They were one of those families who are the backbone of the old West, always ready to serve their neighbors. They were like old trees standing alone on the prairie, that have weathered the storms and grown strong, with their sheltering branches outspread.

When there were signs of a blizzard in the air, it was the Randalls who sent out their sleighs to round up the women who lived alone and bring them in to shelter. When a doctor was needed, the Randalls got one. Young Mrs. Layton was having her first baby sooner than she expected. It was a black night, twenty below zero. The makeshift telephone line was out of order, as it usually was when it was needed.

Mr. Randall called his sons. "You'll have to go for Doc Newman.... Yes, I know it's a bad trip. But you boys know how to take care of yourselves. Make it—if you can." And they rode hell-for-leather.

It seemed to me there never was a time when at least one of the Randalls wasn't riding horseback over the prairie with an urgent message or errand for the homesteaders. Pay? Hell, no! Weren't these newcomers funny!

I remember one evening in January with a storm raging. I had run to the Randalls' house from the print shop. They sent the sleigh to pick up Ida Mary and Wilomene. By dark half a dozen men were marooned at the Halfway House, three of them strangers passing through, three of them plainsmen unable to get home. A little later two homestead women, who had come in from Pierre on the stage and could not go on, joined us.

Somehow there was room for all of them in the big, bare-floored living room. Chairs with an odd assortment of calico-covered cushions were scattered over the room. Crude, old-fashioned tables were set here and there, each with a coal-oil lamp. By the light from the brightly polished chimneys some read newspapers more than a week old, others looked hungrily through the mail-order catalogs which always piled up in country post offices. And Wilomene White, telling some of her homestead anecdotes, filled the room with laughter. Her most harassing experiences seemed funny to Wilomene.

In the middle of the room the big heating stove, stoked with coal, grew red hot as the wind howled and whistled down the chimney and the snow lashed against the windows of the old log house.

Opening off one end of the long room were the small cubicles that served as bedrooms where the women guests would sleep, crowded together, two or three in a bed. Cots would be put up in the living room for the Randall young ones. But the strangers? Leave that to the Randalls—always room for a few more.

"Do you know," said Mr. Randall, "I am never happier than on a night like this, sitting around the fire, knowing my family are all here and safe; and that strangers from out of the storm have found shelter under my roof."

When the weather grew milder and I could ride back and forth again almost daily, it was Mr. Randall who had one of the boys on the ranch wrangle me a range pony which, he said, was "broke" to ride. He *was* broke to ride. The only difficulty was to mount him. It was all right once one got on his back, but only an expert bronco buster could do it. Every time I set foot in the stirrup he went up in the air, pitched, and bucked and sun-fished.

I couldn't draw $10 a week as a printer and waste my time on an outlaw bronc. So I solved it by tying him short with a heavy lariat to the corner post of the hay barn so that he could not get his head up or down, nor his heels up very far. Then I gave one leap into the saddle, Ida cut the rope close to his neck, and away we went to the print shop, where I wrestled with the old, worn-out press. Fortunately, there was no trick to dismounting, although I always expected the worst.

One day I broke loose. I had worked all morning and used up half a can of grease on the press, and still it stuck. I picked up a hammer and tried to break it to pieces. I threw one piece of battered equipment after another across the prairie. ("Don't go near the print shop," a little Randall boy warned all comers; "the printer's a-actin'.")

I scrubbed the ink from my hands and face and boarded the stage. I was off to Presho to meet the proof-sheet king.

E. L. Senn was a magnate in the frontier newspaper field. His career is particularly interesting because it is, in more ways than one, typical of the qualities which made many western men successful. Basically, he was a reformer, a public-spirited man who backed, with every means at his command, and great personal courage, the issues he believed for the good of the country, and fought with equal intensity those which were harmful.

In the early nineties he had moved out to a homestead and started a small cattle ranch. In itself that was a daring gesture, as outlaw gangs—cattle rustlers and horse thieves—infested the region and had become so bold and influential that it was difficult to get any settlers to take up land in it. He started his first newspaper on his homestead, miles from a post office, for the purpose of carrying on his fight with the cattle thieves. In retaliation the outlaws burned him out.

E. L. Senn promptly moved his paper to the nearest post office at a small crossroads station to continue the fight. He incorporated in this paper final proof notices for the settlers. When the fight with the rustlers had been waged to a successful close, he expanded his final-proof business; now he owned the greatest proof-sheet monopoly that ever operated in the West, with a chain of thirty-five papers strung over that part of South Dakota.

As civilization pushed into a new district the king picked up another printing outfit and made entry to the Post Office Department at Washington of another newspaper. Sometimes he moved his own outfits from one region to another, but often he merely shut the door on an old plant not worth moving and let it return to scrap-iron while the print shop tumbled down with it.

It cost a lot of money, he used to complain, with investments depreciating like that and the proof business so short-lived, when the settlers filled a section and all proved up at once. And he had to run a paper a year before it became a legal publication.

But the proof sheets soon became gold mines, the plants costing but a few hundred dollars and the expenses of operating only ten to fifteen dollars a week—a cheap printer, the prints, the ink. Established at inland post offices they became the nuclei for crossroad trading points.

At this time he had embarked on another cause, prohibition, which was causing great excitement in South Dakota. A few years later, with his proof sheets extending through the Black Hills, he bought a newspaper in Deadwood, the notorious old mining town which is usually associated in people's minds with the more lurid aspects of the Wild West. He found conditions all that they had been painted, dominated by underworld vice rings, with twenty-four saloons for its population of 3000, and gambling halls, operated as openly as grocery stores, running twenty-four hours a day. Even the two dance halls exceeded all that has been written about similar places.

With his newspaper as his only weapon E. L. Senn set out to clean up Deadwood. In the fight he sunk his own profits until he had to sell most of his newspapers, emerging from it almost penniless.

It was this doughty warrior whose printing press I had strewn widely over the prairie. When he entered the hotel in Presho where I was awaiting him my courage almost failed me. He was wise enough not to ask me what was wrong. He must have been secretly amused by the very small, frightened girl with the determined expression in her direct blue eyes.

To my surprise, he asked no questions. Instead he took me to supper and then to a moving picture, the first I had seen in the West. His kindness so melted my exasperation with the press that I was at a loss to know how to begin the fighting talk I had come to make. But the film ended with a woman driving sheepmen off her claim, and with that example to fortify my ebbing courage, I asked for a new printing press. And I got it!

The "new" press was a second-hand one, but in comparison to the Noah's Ark model it was a mechanical wonder. I did not know that the proof king was facing a financial crisis at that time. But I've always thought the blow of having to buy a press was not half so bad as the shock of having a printer who would ask for one.

While I was enjoying the new press one day the Reeds came by McClure.

"Well, good-by, folks."

"Oh, are you going?"

"Yes, proved up. Going back to God's country."

God's country to the Reeds was Missouri; to others it was Illinois, or Iowa or Ohio. Day after day homesteaders left with their final receipt as title to their land, pending issuance of a government patent. Throwing back the type of the "dead" notices, I could almost tell who would be pulling out of the country.

"Going back in time to get in the spring crop," farmers would say.

Land grabbers they were called. Taking 160 acres of land with them, and leaving nothing. Most of them never came back.

And while this exodus was taking place, here and there a settler was drifting onto the Lower Brulé, a "lucky number" who had come ahead of time—there was so much to do getting settled. And by these restless signs of change over the plains, we knew that it was spring.

And one week I set up for the paper, "Notice is hereby given that Ida Mary Ammons has filed her intention to make proof...."

VI. "UTOPIA"

With the first tang of spring in the air we cleaned the shack, put up fresh curtains and did a little baking. Then we grew reckless and went into an orgy of extravagance—we took a bath in the washtub. Wash basins were more commensurate with the water supply. Then we scrubbed the floor with the bath water. In one way and another, the settlers managed to develop a million square miles of frontier dirt without a bathtub on it.

For the first time we stopped to take stock, to look ahead. For months there had been time and energy for nothing but getting through the winter. We had been too busy to discuss any plans beyond the proving up.

"What are we going to do after we prove up?" I asked, and Ida Mary shook her head. "I don't know," she admitted.

In some ways it was a relief to have the end in sight. I hated the minute routine of putting a paper together, with one letter of type at a time. I hated the hard mechanical work. Most of our neighbors were proving up, going back. But we realized, with a little shock of surprise, that we did not want to go back. Imperceptibly we had come to identify ourselves with the West; we were a part of its life, it was a part of us. Its hardships were more than compensated for by its unshackled freedom. To go back now would be to make a painful readjustment to city life; it would mean hunting jobs, being tied to the weariness of office routine. The opportunities for a full and active life were infinitely greater here on the prairie. There was a pleasant glow of possession in knowing that the land beneath our feet was ours.

For a little while we faced uncertainly the problem that other homesteaders were facing—that of going back, of trying to fit ourselves in again to city ways. But the eagerness to return to city life had gone. Then, too, there was something in the invigorating winter air and bright sunshine which had given me new resistance. There had been a continuous round of going down, and coming back with a second wind; but I had gained a little each time and was stronger now than before.

In the mid-afternoon, after our orgy of spring house-cleaning, with everything fresh and clean, Ida Mary said, "Someone is coming—straight across our land."

"Who is it?" I asked. We had learned to recognize every horse in that part of the country a mile away. But this was not a plainsman.

We rushed into the shack and made a mad scramble through the trunk, but before we could get dressed there came a knock at the door. "Will you wait a moment, please?" I called. It was the custom of the plains for a man to wait outside while his hostess dressed or put her house in order, there being no corner where he could stay during the process. If the weather prohibited outdoor waiting, he could retire to the hayshed.

A pleasant voice said, "I'll be glad to wait." But as I whispered, "Throw me those slippers," and Ida Mary said *sotto voce*, "What dress shall I wear?" we heard a muffled chuckle through the thin walls.

When we threw open the door to a slightly built man with brown hair and a polished air about him, I knew it was the cartoonist from Milwaukee. Only a city man and an artist could look like that.

"How do you do, Mr. Van Leshout."

"How did you know?" he said, as he came in.

"So you were a Lucky Number, after all," seemed a more appropriate response than telling him that it was spring and something had been bound to happen, something like the arrival of a cartoonist from Milwaukee.

"Are you going to be a settler?" Ida Mary asked doubtfully.

He laughed. Yes, he had taken a homestead close to the Sioux settlement so that he could paint some Indian pictures.

Odd how we kept forgetting the Indians, but up to now we hadn't even seen one, nor were we likely to, we thought, barricaded as they were in their own settlement. "But they are wonderful," he assured us enthusiastically; "magnificent people to paint; old, seamed faces and some really beautiful young ones. Character, too, and glamor!"

We invited him to tea, but he explained that he must get back to his claim before dark. It was already too late, Imbert told him; he would have to wait for the moon to rise. Imbert had dropped in, as he had a habit of doing, and seeing him through the eyes of an easterner we realized what fascination the lives of these plainsmen had for city men.

In honor of the occasion we got out the china cups, a wanton luxury on the plains, and tea and cake. As they rode off, Van Leshout called to us: "Come over to the shack. I built it myself. You'll know it by the crepe on the door."

As the two men melted into the darkness we closed the door reluctantly against the soft spring air. Strange that we had found prairie life dull!

One morning soon after the unexpected appearance of the Milwaukee cartoonist I awoke to find the prairie in blossom. Only in the spring is there color over that great expanse; but for a few weeks the grass is green and the wild flowers bloom in delicate beauty—anemones, tiny white and yellow and pink blossoms wherever the eye rests. I galloped to the print shop with the wind blowing through my hair, rejoicing in the sudden beauty, and found myself too much in holiday mood to get to work.

Suddenly I looked up from the type case to find an arresting figure in the doorway, a middle-aged man with an air of power and authority about him.

"I'm waiting for the stage," he said. "May I come in?"

I offered him the only chair there was—an upturned nail keg—and he sat down.

"Where do you come from?" he asked abruptly.

"St. Louis," I said.

"But why come out here to run a newspaper?"

"I didn't. I came to homestead with my sister, but the job was here."

Because he was amused at the idea, because the function of these frontier papers seemed unimportant to him, I began to argue the point, and finally, thoroughly aroused, described the possibilities which grew in my own mind as I discussed them. There was a tremendous job for the frontier newspaper to do, I pointed out. Did he know the extent of this great homestead movement and the future it promised? True, the frontier papers were small in size, but they could become a power in the development of this raw country.

"How?" he demanded.

I think I fully realized it for the first time myself then. "As a medium of cooperation," I told him.

He got up and walked to the window, hands in pockets, and looked out over the prairie. Then he turned around. "But the development of this country is a gigantic enterprise," he protested. "It would require the backing of corporations and millions of dollars. In fact, it's too big for any organization but the government to tackle. It's no job for a woman." His eyes twinkled as he contrasted my diminutive size with the great expanse of undeveloped plains. "What could you do?"

"Of course it's big," I admitted, "and the settlers do need lots of money. But they need cooperation, too. Their own strength, acting together, counts more than you know. And a newspaper could be made a voice for these people."

"Utopian," he decided.

Bill appeared at the door to tell him that "The stage has been a-waitin' ten minutes, now."

He handed me his card, shook hands and rushed out. I looked at the card: "Halbert Donovan and Company, Brokers, Investment Bankers, New York City." The fact that such men were coming into the country, looking it over, presaged development. Not only the eyes of the landseekers but those of industry and finance were turning west.

I stared after the stagecoach until it was swallowed up in distance. My own phrases kept coming back to me. There was a job to be done, a job for a frontier newspaper, and soon the McClure *Press* would be a thing of the past—as soon as the homesteaders had made proof. Slowly an idea was taking shape.

I slammed the print-shop door shut, mounted Pinto and loped home. I turned the horse loose to graze and walked into the shack.

With my back against the door in a defensive attitude I said abruptly, "I'm going to start a newspaper on the reservation."

Ida Mary slowly put down the bread knife. "But where are you going to get the money?" she asked practically.

"I don't know, yet. I have to plan what to do first, don't I, and then look around for a way to do it." That was the formula followed day after day by the settlers.

"It's too bad you didn't register for a claim in the Drawing," she said thoughtfully. "After all, there is no reason why you shouldn't have a claim too."

"I could still get a homestead on the Brulé," I declared, "and I can run the newspaper on the homestead."

The more we discussed the plan the more Ida Mary liked the idea of moving to the Strip where so many new people would be coming. We would work together, we planned, and the influence of the newspaper would radiate all over the reservation. But, it occurred to us, coming abruptly down to earth, with no roads or telephones or mail service, how were the settlers to receive the radiation?

This was a stickler, but having gone so far with our plans we were reluctant to abandon them. Where there was a newspaper there should be a post office. Then we would start a post office! Through it the land notices would be received and the newspaper mailed to the subscribers. The settlers could get the paper and their mail at the same place. We decided that Ida Mary would run it. Somehow it did not occur to us that the government has something to say about post offices and who shall run them. Or that the government might not want to put a post office on my homestead just to be obliging.

But once a person has learned to master difficulties as they come up, he begins to feel he can handle anything; so Ida took her final proof receipt to a loan office in Presho.

"How much can I borrow on this?" she asked, handing it to the agent.

"Oh, about eight hundred dollars."

"That isn't enough. Most homesteaders are getting a thousand-dollar loan when they prove up."

"Yes, but your land's a mile long and only a quarter wide—"

Ida Mary was not easily bluffed. She reached for the receipt. "I'll try Sedgwick at the bank."

"We'll make it nine hundred," the agent said, "but not a cent more. I know that quarter section; it's pretty rough."

Homesteading was no longer a precarious venture. A homesteader could borrow $1000 on almost any quarter-section in the West—more on good land, well located. It was a criminal offense to sell or mortgage government land, but who could wait six months or a year for the government to issue a patent (deed) to the land? Many of the settlers must borrow money to make proof. So the homestead loan business became a sleight-of-hand performance.

The homesteader could not get this receipt of title until he paid the Land Office for the land, and he could not pay for the land until he had the receipt to turn over to the loan agent. So it was all done simultaneously—money, mortgages, final-proof receipts; like juggling half a dozen balls in the air at once. It was one of the most ingenious methods of finance in operation. Banks and loan companies went into operation to handle homestead loans, and eastern capital began flowing in for the purpose.

Being familiar with Land Office procedure from my work on the McClure *Press*, I knew that not every winner of a claim on the Lower Brulé reservation would come to prove it up. A few of them would relinquish their rights. The buying and selling of relinquishments, in fact, became a big business for the land agents. There was a mad rush for relinquishments on the Strip, where landseekers were paying as high as $1000 to $1200 for the right to file on a claim.

I wanted a relinquishment on the reservation, in the very center of it, and I found one for $400.

Then I made a deal with a printing equipment firm for a small plant—a new one! And, although there were only a dozen settlers or so on the land, I pledged 400 proof notices as collateral.

These proofs at $5 apiece were as sure as government bonds; that is, if the settlers on the Brulé stayed long enough to prove up, if the newspaper lived, and if no one else started a paper in competition. But on that score the printers' supply company was satisfied. Its officers thought there was no danger of anyone else trailing an outfit into that region.

We arranged for straight credit on lumber for a print shop, there being nothing left to mortgage. From now on we were dealing in futures. In just two short weeks I had become a reckless plunger, aided and abetted by Ida Mary. The whole West was gambling on the homesteaders' making good.

Long we hesitated over the letter home, telling of our new plans. Under the new laws, one must stay on a claim fourteen months, instead of the eight months required when Ida Mary had filed. At last we wrote to explain that we were not coming home this spring. We were going on to a new frontier.

Earnestly as we believed in the plans we had made, it was hard to make that letter carry our convictions, difficult to explain the logic of our moving to an Indian reservation so that Ida Mary could run a non-existent post office in order to mail copies of a non-existent newspaper to non-existent settlers. Looking at it like that, we were acting in blind faith.

And one day a funny little caravan made its way across the prairie, breaking a new trail as it went. A shack with a team hitched to it, a wagon loaded with immigrant goods; and a printing press; ahead, leading the way, a girl on horseback.

Again it was Huey Dunn who jacked up our old shack that morning when the term of school was over and put it on wheels for the trip to the reservation—twelve miles around by McClure, a few miles closer by a short-cut across the plains. Huey decided on the latter way, and I rode on ahead to see that the load of printing equipment should be put on the right quarter-section, while Ida Mary came in the shack. She sat in the rocking chair, gazing placidly out of the window as it made its way slowly across the plains.

We had hired two homesteaders to haul out lumber and put up a small building for the newspaper and post office, although we had not yet got the necessary petition signed for a post office. We could not do that before the settlers arrived. A small shed room was built a few feet from the business structure as a lean-to for our migratory shack.

When I arrived at the claim the men who had hauled out the load of equipment were gone. Suddenly there came on one of those torrential downpours that often deluge the dry plains in spring. It was pitch black as night came on, and no sight of Huey and Ida Mary. The rain stopped at length. Throwing on a sweater, I paced back and forth through the dripping grass listening for the sound of the horses. At last I went back and crouched over the fire in the little lean-to, waiting. There was nothing else I could do.

At midnight Huey arrived with the shack. He and Ida Mary were cold and wet and hungry. They had not had a bite to eat since early morning. Just as they had reached Cedar Creek, usually a little dry furrow in the earth, a flood of water came rushing in a torrent, making a mad, swollen stream that spread rapidly, and they were caught in it. When they got in the middle of the stream the shack began to fill with water. Huey grabbed Ida Mary and got her on one horse while he mounted the other, and the horses swam to land.

The next morning the sun came out, flooding the new-washed plains. It was a different world from the harsh, drab prairie to which we had come eight months ago. Here the earth was a soft green carpet, heavily sprinkled with spring flowers, white and lavender hyacinths, bluebells, blossoms flaming red, yellow and blue, and snow-white, waxen flowers that wither at the touch and yet bloom on the hard desert.

Huey Dunn squared the migratory shack and rolled the wheels from under. And there in the Land of the Burnt Thigh, the Indians' name for the Brulé, I filed my claim and started a newspaper. The only woman, so it was recorded, ever to establish a newspaper on an Indian reservation. And if one were to pick up the first issues of that newspaper he would see under the publisher's name, "Published on Section 31, Township 108 North, Range 77W, of the 5th Principal Meridian," the only way of describing its location.

Ida's claim had seemed to us at first sight to be in the midst of nowhere. Compared to this, it had been in a flourishing neighborhood. For here there was nothing but the land—waiting. No sign of habitation, no living thing—yes, an antelope standing rigid against the horizon. For a terrified moment it seemed that there could be no future here—only time. And Ida Mary and I shrank from two very confident young women to two very young and frightened girls.

But there was work to be done. Our tar-covered cabin sat parallel to and perhaps ten feet from the drop-siding print shop—a crude store building 12 × 24 feet, which we called the Brulé business block. We had a side door put on near the back end of each building so that we could slip easily from house to shop. We did a little remodeling of our old shack. Befitting our new position as business leaders, we built a 6 × 8 shed-roof kitchen onto the back of the shack and a clothes closet in one end of it; we even bought a little cookstove with an oven in it.

One morning we saw a team and wagon angling across the Strip toward our place. Upon the top of the wagon there perched a high rectangular object, a funny-looking thing, bobbing up and down as the wagon jolted over the rough ground. It was Harvey with the outhouse. There was nothing left now on Ida Mary's claim but the mortgage.

Confronted suddenly by so many problems of getting started, I stood "just plumb flabbergasted," as Coyote Cal, a cowpuncher, always remarked when unexpectedly confronted by a group of women.

And yet I knew what I wanted to do. I had known since the day I heard myself telling the New York broker. An obscure little newspaper in a desolate homestead country: but, given courage enough, that little printing outfit would be a tool, a voice for the people's needs. It was a gigantic task, this taming of the frontier.

And meantime, getting down to reality, I had a newspaper without a country, without a living thing but prairie dogs and rattlesnakes to read it. And around us a hundred thousand acres on which no furrow had ever been turned.

We did not know where to begin. There wasn't a piece of kindling wood on the whole reservation. We had brought what food and water we could with us. Food, fuel, water. Those were basic problems that had to be met.

And then, within a week, almost imperceptibly, a change began to come over the reservation. The Lucky Numbers were coming onto the land. On the claim to the west a house went up and wagons of immigrant goods were unloaded. Ida Mary rode over one evening and found that our new neighbor was a farmer, Christopher Christopherson, from Minnesota. He had brought plows and work horses and was ready to break sod, another example of the farmers who were leaving the settled states for cheap land farther west.

Mrs. Christopherson was a thrifty Swedish farm woman who would manage well. There was a big family of children, and each child old enough to work was given work to do.

Around us new settlers were arriving daily and we felt that the time had come to start out among them with our post-office petition. With Pinto as our only means of transportation it proved to be a slow job.

One day, dropping suddenly down off the tableland into a draw, I came squarely upon a shack. I rode up, and an old white-whiskered man invited me in. His wife, a gray-haired, sharp-featured woman, appeared to me much younger than he. I explained my errand.

"For mercy sake," the woman said, "here you are starting a post office and I thought you was one of them high-falutin' city homesteaders a rec-connoiterin' around. Listen to that, Pa, a post office in four miles of us."

The woman put out a clean cup and plate. "Set up," she said. "We ain't signing any petition till you've had your dinner. There's plenty of biscuit. I stirred up an extry cup of flour and I said to Pa, 'They'll be et!'"

I ate salt pork, biscuit and sorghum while she talked.

65

"So you're going to handle newspapers too. Oh, print one!" She sighed. "Seems to me that would be a pestiferous job. We're going to have a newspaper out here, Pa, did you ever—?" Pa never did.

Where had I seen these two old people before, and heard this woman talk?

"Where you from?" she asked, but before I could answer, she went on, "We're from Blue Springs."

Pa wrote "David H. Wagor" on the petition.

One morning Imbert Miller came with his team and buggy to take us out into a more remote district to get signers. We found two or three farmers, a couple of business men with their families, and several young bachelors, each building the regular rough-lumber shack. They were surprised and elated over the prospect of a post office.

After wandering over a long vacant stretch, Imbert began to look for a place where he could feed the horses and get us some food. At last we saw bright new lumber glistening in the sun. As we drove up to the crudely built cabin we saw an emblem painted on the front—a big black circle with the letter V in it, and underneath, the word "Rancho." Standing before the open doorway was an easel with a half-finished Indian head on it.

"Van Leshout's!" Ida Mary exclaimed.

He came out, unshaven, and sweeping an old paint-daubed hat from his head with a low bow. "It's been years since I saw a human being," he exclaimed. "You'll want grub."

Building a cabin, learning to prepare his own meals, getting accustomed to solitude were new experiences for the cartoonist from Milwaukee.

"Not many courses," he said, as he dragged the spuds out from under the bunk; "just two—b'iled potatoes, first course; flapjacks and 'lasses, second course; and coffee."

"You've discovered the Indians," we said, pointing to the canvas.

The Indians, yes, but they hadn't been much of a cure for loneliness. What were we doing on the reservation?

We brought out the post-office petition and told him about the newspaper. I explained that I had filed on a claim on the reservation.

"I looked for the crepe on the door as we drove up," I told him.

"You have a claim on the reservation? To hell with the crepe!" he said in high spirits.

On the road home, seeing Imbert's elation, it occurred to me that I had never taken into consideration the fact that Imbert Miller lived near the borders of the reservation and that the "fence" would not separate him from Ida Mary now. How deeply she had weighed the question I did not know.

We sent in the post-office petition and the federal authorities promptly established a post office for the Lower Brulé on my homestead and appointed Ida Mary postmistress. She was the only woman ever to run a post office on an Indian reservation, the data gatherers said. The government named it Ammons.

So we had a postmistress and a post office, with its tiers of empty, homemade pigeonholes ready to receive the mail.

And we discovered there was no way to get any mail in or out!

VII. BUILDING EMPIRES
OVERNIGHT

That spring I saw a country grow. Perhaps Rome wasn't built in a day, but the Brulé was—almost. The incredible speed of the transformation of the untouched plains; the invasion of the settlers in droves, lighting on the prairies like grasshoppers; the appearance, morning after morning, of new shacks, as though they had sprung up overnight; the sound of hammers echoing through the clear, light air; plows at last tearing at the unbroken ground—the wonder of it leaves me staggered now, but then I was caught up in the breathless rush, the mad activity to get things done. The Lucky Numbers were coming, coming.

A few weeks before, we had set up our shack in a wilderness. Now there were shacks everywhere and frantic activity. The plains had come to life. Over them, where there had been bleak emptiness, loomed tents, white against the green background, where the settlers could sleep until they were able to build houses. There was no time to rest, no time to pause—here where there had been nothing but time.

Late one evening a wagon loaded with immigrant goods and a shabby car loaded with children passed our place. The drivers stopped on a nearby claim, threw their bedding on the ground, and slept there. Their deadline for establishing residence was up that night. All over the plains that intensive race went on, the hurried arrival of settlers before their time should expire, the hasty throwing up of shelter against the weather, the race to plant crops in the untamed soil so that there would be food later on.

A land where one must begin at the beginning! Everything to be done, and things crying to be done all at once. Those three basic needs, food, fuel, water—problems which must be solved without delay.

Moving in a network, criss-cross in every direction, wagons and teams hauled in immigrant goods, lumber and machinery, fence posts and fuel; post holes supplemented those dug by the prairie dogs; strings of barb-wire ran threadlike over the unbroken stretch.

From day to day we saw the prairie change, saw new, crude houses thrown up, saw the first furrows broken in the stubborn soil, saw men and women pit themselves against the frontier and shape it to their purpose and their needs.

Among these people there were many more dirt farmers than had settled around McClure, but at least 50 per cent of the immigrants were young men and women from various walks of life, business and professions, who had come for health or adventure; or because the land, through sale or mortgage, would give them a start in life. While it is doubtless true that these latter contributed little to the permanent building of the West, the zest with which they enjoyed its advantages, the gallantry with which they faced its hardships, contributed no small part to increasing the morale of the settlers as a whole.

Almost every settler scooped out a dam at the foot of a slope for water supply. We had Chris Christopherson plow one for us. These dams were nothing but waterholes twelve to fifteen feet in diameter and two or three feet deep. There should be late spring rains to fill them for the summer. There were! While the settlers were still plowing and planting and making their dams it began to rain. And when the frontier is wet, it's wet all over. Dry creeks swelled to overflowing, and small ravines became creeks, and it kept on raining. Both Ida

Mary and I were caught in one of those downpours and had to swim the horses across swift-rising Cedar Creek.

Much of those first days were like chapters from Genesis, and to add to the similarity we now had the Flood! The seed shot out of the ground and the fields were green. The gardens grew like Jack's beanstalk. The thick grass stood a foot high. And the dams were full of water.

And Ida Mary and I were literally in the center of this maze of activity, this mushroom growth of a country. And Ammons was actually on the map!

My sister wrote to the Postal Department for a mail carrier and found out she would have to solve that problem for herself.

"We aren't cut out to cope with the plains," I said.

"How did you happen to find that out?" asked Ida Mary.

"I didn't. A New York broker told me."

We had to find some way to get mail in and out. We couldn't back up on the trail, once we had started. There was no place to back to. So we bought a team and started a U. S. mail route, hauling mail three times a week from the stage line at McClure.

It was the thing that had to be done, but sometimes, when we had a moment for reflection, we were a little aghast. Carrying a mail route in homestead country was a far cry from life in St. Louis. It began to seem as though we rarely acted according to plan out here; rather, we were acted upon by unforeseen factors, so that our activities were constantly shifting, taking on new form, leading in new directions. The only consistent thing about them was that they never back-trailed!

Now and then we hired boys to help us with heavy jobs which were beyond our strength, and occasionally a young prairie girl, Ada Long, fourteen years old, went for the mail. It was against the law to let anyone who happened to be handy carry the mail, but the settlers had to have postal service.

Ada was fair, with long yellow braids, strong and accustomed to the hard ways of the prairie. She could hitch up a team and drive it like a man. There was only one drawback to Ada. On Saturday when we were busiest she went home and to church; and on Sunday she hung out the washing. Ada was a loyal Adventist.

Settlers meeting on the trail hailed one another with "Hello! Where you from? I'm from Illinois"—or Virginia—or Iowa. "You breakin'?" They had no time for backgrounds. It didn't matter what the newcomers might have been. That was left beyond the reservation gate. One's standing was measured by what he could do and what kind of neighbor he would make. And always the question, "Where you from?" Missouri, Michigan, Wisconsin.

Bronco Benny, riding through one day, said, "I never seen so many gals in my life. Must be a trainload of 'em. Some pretty high-headed fillies among 'em, too." Bronco Benny knew no other language than that of the horse world in which he lived.

Not only dirt farmers but many others became sodbreakers. The sod was heavy, and with the great growth of grass it took all the strength of man and teams, four to six horses hitched to a plow, to turn it. Steady, slow, furrow by furrow, man and beast dripping with sweat, they broke fields of the virgin earth.

How deep to plow, how to cultivate this land, few of them knew. The more experienced farmers around the Strip, like Huey Dunn, would know. Here was a service the newspaper could perform by printing such information for the newcomers. Subscriptions for the paper began coming in before we were ready to print it. We named it *The Reservation Wand*, and how it ever was accepted in that man's country with a name like that is beyond me. The first issue was distributed by homesteaders passing by and two carriers.

Subscriptions came in rapidly at a dollar a year. Not only did most of the settlers subscribe, but they put in subscriptions for friends and relatives, so that these might know something of the country and its activities. And in their rush of getting settled it was easier to have the printer set up the news and run it off on a press than to take the time to write a letter. Outsiders could not send in subscriptions by mail until the newspaper had an address other than a section number of the claim on which it was printed.

Food, shelter, fuel were still the pressing problems. An army had peopled a land without provisions. Trade was overwhelmed and the small towns could not get supplies shipped in fast enough. New business enterprises were following this rush as lightning does a lightning rod. There was bedlam. One could not get a plowshare sharpened, a bolt, or a bushel of coal without making the long trip to town. One could not get a pound of coffee or a box of matches on the whole reservation.

The settlers began to clamor for a store in connection with the newspaper and the post office. Their needs ran more to coffee and sugar and nails than to newspapers. They had to have a store for a few essential commodities at least.

A store? I objected strenuously. We had already embarked on enough enterprises, and running a store had no place among them. But practical Ida was really interested in the project. It wasn't such a bad idea, she decided. Our money was dwindling, the newspaper would not become a paying proposition for some time, and the only revenue from the post office was the meager cancellation of stamps.

We could hire the hauling done, she pointed out, grappling at once with the details. And it would be a real service to the settlers. That was what we had wanted to provide—the means didn't matter so much.

So we planked down a cash payment at a wholesale-retail store at Presho for a bill of goods, got credit for the rest of it, threw up an ell addition on the back of the shop for the newspaper, and stuck a grocery store where the newspaper had been.

All this time we had been so submerged in activities connected with getting settled, starting and operating a newspaper, a post office, and now a store, that we had overlooked a rather important point—that on an Indian reservation one might reasonably expect Indians. We had forgotten the Indians.

And one afternoon they came. On horseback and in wagons, war bonnets and full regalia glittering in the sun, the Indians were coming straight toward the Ammons settlement. Neither of us had ever seen an Indian outside of a Wild West show.

We were terrified. Into the shack we scurried, locked doors and windows, and peeped out through a crack in the drawn blind.

The Indians had stopped and turned their horses loose to graze. We could hear them walking around the store and print shop—and then came savage mutterings outside our door and heavy pounding. We crawled under the bed. A woman we knew had escaped being scalped once by hiding behind a shock of corn. But there was no such refuge here.

"How! How kill 'em?" an old Indian was bellowing. No use trying to escape. This was the end.

Trembling, hearts pounding, we opened the door. Two big savage-looking creatures with battered faces stood there motioning toward the shop where a group of them were sauntering in and out.

"How kill 'em?" they still muttered. Dazed, we followed them. They had taken possession of the shop. Women were sitting on the floor, some with papooses strapped to their backs. Men with hair hanging loose, or braided down their backs, tied with red string, were picking up everything in the print shop, playing like children with new toys.

They led us into the store, muttering, "*Shu-hum-pah; she-la,*" as they pointed to the shelves. At last we found they wanted sugar and tobacco, and we lost no time in filling the order.

At sunset they rode away toward the Indian settlement, and we discovered that we had been misled by the talk of "segregation." To us that had meant that the Indians were behind some high barricade. But there wasn't a thing to separate us from the tribe but another barb-wire fence, with the gates down.

For several days after the red men came we moved in a nightmare of fear. The Sioux had cherished this tall grass country as a hunting ground, and we had invaded it. Suppose they were intent upon revenge!

Then, absorbed in our many duties, we almost forgot about the Indians. But a week after their first visit they came again. They arrived shortly before sundown, adorned in beads and feathers, stopped across the trail, and to our horror pitched camp. Pinto commenced to neigh and kept it up, a restless whinny, eager for his own people.

It looked as though the whole Sioux tribe had moved over to Ammons. While the men unhitched and unsaddled, the squaws—for the most part large shapeless creatures totally unlike the slim Indian maid of fiction, and indescribably dirty—started small fires with twigs they had brought with them. By now Ma Wagor, the gray-haired woman from Blue Springs, was in the store every day, helping out, and she was as terrified as Ida and I. It seems there were no Indians in Blue Springs. They were among the few contingencies for which Ma Wagor was not amply prepared.

By chance a strange cowboy came through about sundown and stopped for a package of tobacco. While he dexterously rolled a cigarette with one hand we surrounded him, three panic-stricken women. Did he think the Indians were on the war path, we asked, our teeth chattering.

"Oh, I don't know," he answered carelessly, "can't tell a speck about an Indian. Couldn't blame 'em, could you, with these landgrabbers invadin' their range?"

The logic of this had already occurred to us, and we were not particularly cheered by the cowboy's confirmation of our worst suspicions.

"What do you suppose they're buildin' them fires for?" Ma Wagor was anxious to know.

Sourdough couldn't say as to that. But he 'lowed it might be to burn the scalps in.

At that we missed Ma. She had slipped into the house to wash her feet. Ma was a great believer in preparedness, whether having something cooked ahead for supper, or clean feet for heaven.

Instinctively I put my hand on my shock of fair hair to make sure it was still in place. It had always been a nuisance, but now I felt a passionate eagerness to keep it where it was.

The Indians stretched their tepees and cooked their supper. The prairie around them was alive with bony horses and hungry-looking dogs. It was the impatient yelping of the dogs about the kettles rather than any sounds from the soft-footed Indians which we heard.

The cowboy threw his cigarette on the floor, stamped on it with a jingle of spurs, and drawled, "Guess I'll be percolatin'—got to ride night-herd."

Ma Wagor grabbed him by his wide belt. "You're goin' to do your night-herdin' right in front of this shack," she declared grimly. "You've got your pistol and we women need protection." Looking at Ma's set jaw he promised to hang around that night.

Locked in the shack, we waited for the cowboy's signal of attack. He'd "shoot 'em down as fast as they crossed the trail," he assured us, but we were not so confident of his prowess.

"I'd send for Pa," Ma Wagor said dismally, "but what good would he do? And one of us has got to be left to prove up the claim." It was unlikely, according to Ma, that anyone in that cabin would survive. But as the night wore on everything across the trail became quiet and at last we threw ourselves across the bed, exhausted. We woke next morning to find our cowboy gone and the Indians cooking breakfast.

Two leather-skinned men with hair hanging loose over their shoulders and faces painted in red and copper hues led a big-boned horse up to the door and walked into the store. They pointed to the shelves, held up ten fingers, then pointed to the horse. They wanted to trade it for ten dollars' worth of groceries.

Ida Mary did not bother to look at the horse. She traded. The last thing that would have occurred to her at that moment was to disagree with any wishes the Indians might express. We found out later that the old mare was stone-blind and locoed.

Within a week we had the corral full of horses—the lame, the halt and the blind. We would have traded the whole store for anything that the Indians wanted, to get rid of them.

Sourdough, who belonged to the Scotty Phillips outfit over on the Indian lands, had ridden straight on to do night-herd duty. Every cowpuncher, it seemed, must play at least one trick on the tenderfeet.

Then one day a handsomely built young buck, straight as an arrow, walked into the print shop. "How Kola!" he said, and then introduced himself as Joe Two-Hawk. He was a college graduate, it appeared, and he explained that "How Kola" was the friendly greeting of the Sioux, a welcome to the two white girls who ran the settlement.

Many of these young Indians went East to Indian colleges, acquiring, along with their education, a knowledge of civilized ways to which they adapted themselves with amazing rapidity. On returning to the reservations, however, in many cases, perhaps in most, they discarded one by one, as though they had never been, the ways of the white man, and reverted to their primitive customs and ways of life. Nor should they be too thoughtlessly condemned for it. Among civilized peoples the same urge for an escape from responsibility exists, thwarted often enough merely by necessity, or by the pressure of convention and public opinion. The Indians who have reverted to type, discarded the ways of civilization for a tepee and primitive uncleanliness, follow the path of least resistance. Traditions of accomplishment as we know them have no meaning for the Indians; and the way of life for which his own traditions have fitted him has been denied him.

How Kola! That must be what the old warrior was bellowing the day we thought he had said he would kill us. Old Two-Hawk laughed at that when his son Joe interpreted it in Sioux.

Old Two-Hawk explained us to his son, of whom he was manifestly very proud. He pointed to me. "He-paleface-prints-paper"; then to Ida Mary, "Him-paleface-trades-horses." Thus the Brulé Indians distinguished us from each other.

Joe Two-Hawk had come as a sort of emissary from the Brulés. They wanted us, he explained, to make Ammons an Indian trading post. Looking at the corral, we felt, to our sorrow, that they had already done so. Joe Two-Hawk said they had wood and berries in abundance along the Missouri River, which ran through the Indian lands. They wanted to exchange them for merchandise. And the settlers, we knew, needed the Indian commodities.

So to the newspaper, the post office, the store, the mail route, the heavy hauling, we added an Indian trading post, trading groceries for fence posts; subscriptions to *The Wand* for berries—very few of them could read it, but they didn't mind that—it was a trade. Joe Two-Hawk became a mediator and interpreter until Ida Mary and I learned enough of the Sioux language to carry on. We tried to figure out a way, in this trading, to make back our loss on the menagerie we had collected at Ammons. Those bare store shelves worried us. Then, one morning, the old, blind, locoed mare turned up with a fine colt by her side. We were getting even.

And we no longer minded that the gate was open between the Indian lands and the section of the Brulé which had been thrown open to white settlers. While the gate stood open, enmity and mutual suspicion could not exist, and the path between it and Ammons was beaten hard and smooth.

The Indians came in processions with loaded wagons; unloaded, turned their horses loose on the range and sat around—men and women—for hours at a time on floor or ground, dickering. Ida Mary became as expert at it as they were. It was not long before *The Wand* had legal work from them, the settling of estates, notices pertaining to land affairs, etc. And that led, logically enough, to Ida Mary's being appointed a notary public.

"Want to sell your land, girls?" a man from Presho asked us one day. "That's what I drove out for. I have a buyer anxious to get a claim on the Brulé and I believe he would pay $1200 for this relinquishment. A quick profit."

"Sell? No!" we declared. "With such demand for land on the Strip we may be able to get $2500 for it when it is proved up."

He agreed. A raw quarter-section of deeded land just outside the border had sold the other day for $3500, he informed us. With all the breaking and improvement going on over the Brulé, it was predicted by real-estate boosters that choice homesteads here would be worth $4000 to $5000 in another year or so—after the land was deeded.

Within sixty days after the arrival of the first Lucky Number on his claim the 200 square miles of the Brulé would be filled. The winners had filed consecutively, so many numbers each day for that length of time. Their time to establish residence would thus expire accordingly. Already the broad expanse of grassland we had seen during our first week on the Brulé was changed beyond recognition, shacks everywhere, fields plowed, movement and activity. The frontier had receded once more before the advancing tide of civilization. Within sixty days!

With the price of claims soaring, it became a mecca for claim jumpers. They circled around ready to light on the land like buzzards on a carcass. They watched every quarter-section for the arrival of the settler. If he were not on his land by dark of the last day, some "spotter" was likely to jump the claim and next morning rush to the Land Office and slap a contest on it.

They were unlike the claim jumpers of the older pioneer days who jumped the land because they wanted it for a home. Many of these men would not have proved up a claim at any price. But in many instances they brought landseekers with them who legally filed contests and homesteading rights over the settler. They paid the claim jumpers well for their services in getting hold of the land. Often, being strangers, the landseekers did not know that these "spotters" were not land agents.

They were a ruthless lot as a whole, these claim jumpers. They took long chances, illegally selling relinquishments and skipping the country before they were caught. Some of them even threatened or intimidated newcomers who knew nothing about the West or its land laws.

Of a different type were unscrupulous locating agents who used the technicalities of the homestead law to operate the despicable "contest" business. Whether they had any grounds for contesting a homestead or not, they could claim they had, and the settler must then either go to trial to defend his rights or give up the land. It was a serious problem for the settlers.

So many strangers came and went that the homesteaders seldom identified these land thieves, but the print shop, set high in the middle of the plains, was like a ranger's lookout where we could watch their maneuvers; they traveled in rickety cars or with team and buggy, often carrying camping equipment with them. By the way they drove or rode back and forth, we could spot the "spotters."

They often stopped at the settlement for tobacco or a lunch out of the store—and a little information.

"Whose shack is that off to the southwest?" a man asked one morning, reading off the claim numbers from a slip of paper. He was a ruddy-faced man dressed in a baggy checkered suit with a heavy gold watch chain across the front of his vest and a big flashy ring.

"Belongs to a woman from Missouri," Ida Mary told him. "She had a neighbor build the shack for her."

"No one living there," he said.

"Oh, yes," Ida Mary improvised rapidly, "she was in here yesterday on the way to town for furniture. Won't be back until tomorrow night."

He looked doubtful. "Doesn't look to me as though anyone ever slept there. Not a thing in the shack—no bed."

Ida Mary called out to me, "Edith, didn't you lend that woman some bedding yesterday?"

"Yes," I declared, "so she could sleep there a few nights before the deadline."

All our early training in truth-telling was lost in the skirmish, and sometimes I doubted if the truth was left in us. But there was zest in this outwitting of men who would have defrauded the settlers if they could.

One day I noticed two men driving back and forth over a vacant claim nearby. At sundown no one had established residence. I watched the maneuvers of the two men.

"Ida," I called, "those men are going to jump that claim."

I looked over my land plat and saw that the homestead belonged to Rosie Carrigan from Ohio. It was the last day of grace. She had until midnight to get there.

It was a moonlight night. Ida Mary saddled Pinto and rode down the draw toward the claim. From a slope where she could not be seen she watched the two men. The evening wore on. At eleven o'clock, secure in the knowledge that the owner had failed to arrive, the men pitched camp.

Ida Mary rode quietly up the draw and galloped up to the cabin. "They are sleeping on the claim," she said breathlessly. This meant that next morning, as soon as the Land Office opened, one of them would be there to slap a contest on the land, while the other held possession. It also meant that when Rosie Carrigan arrived she would find her homestead gone.

"What shall we do?" I asked anxiously.

Ida Mary considered for a moment. "One of us must be Rosie Carrigan," she decided. She ran out to hitch the team to the wagon while I hurriedly dragged a few things out of the house and loaded them—things such as an immigrant must carry with him, bedding, boxes, a traveling bag or two. We threw them in the wagon, circled off a mile or two, and then drove straight back onto the land. A few rods from the claim-jumpers we drove a stake, hung a lantern on it, and began to unhitch, shivering with excitement and apprehension.

The noise of our arrival roused the two men, who stirred, and then with an exclamation got to their feet. We saw the flare of a match. One of them had drawn out his watch and was looking at it. Under the smoked-lantern light we looked at ours—it was ten minutes to twelve!

We heard them murmur to each other, but continued unhitching the horses, dragging the hastily assembled articles out of the wagon. Then my heart began to pound. One of the men walked over to us. He was short, burly, heavy-jawed.

"Here, you can't stay here! Where do you think you are?" he demanded.

We made no answer, but the bed I contrived to make under his watching eyes was a hopeless tangle.

"We're on this land...." he blustered. He was trying to run a bluff, to find out whether we were on the right quarter-section or whether, like him, we were land-grabbers.

"I guess I'll have to have your identification," he said again. "What's your name?"

"Rosie Carrigan," I answered, "from Ohio. What are you doing on my land, anyway? You have no right here!"

He hesitated, weighing the situation and the possibilities.

"Get off!" I blazed at him.

He got. The two men rolled up their bedding and moved on, and Ida Mary and I sat limply on the ground watching them go.

In case they should come back we decided to hold the land for the night, gathered up the bedding, and slept in the wagon—when we slept.

At daybreak we were wakened by the rumble of a heavy-loaded wagon coming slowly over the prairie behind a limping team. A tall, slim girl and a slight boy sat high on the front seat. They drove up beside our wagon. Fastened on the back of their load was a chicken coop, and as they stopped a rooster stuck its head out and crowed.

The girl was Rosie Carrigan. The boy was her brother. And the rooster was the first of his kind to settle on the reservation. They had been delayed by footsore horses. But no land-grabbers, no one except ourselves, ever knew that Rosie Carrigan did not establish residence at ten minutes before midnight.

Not long after this, a rough-looking stranger rode up to an old man's shack and took some papers out of his pocket. "There's some mistake here, pardner," he said. "Looks like you're on the wrong quarter. This is section—" he read the description, "and it happens to be mine."

"But that's the number of the claim I filed on at the Drawing," the old man assured him.

After much arguing and bullying, with the old man contending he was right, the stranger ordered him off the land.

"You don't pull that stuff on me, pardner; you'd better vacate."

"Now keep your shirt on, stranger," the old man said, with a twitching of his long white mustache, inviting him in for a bite to eat while he hunted up his land receipts.

"I'm all crippled up with the rheumatiz," he groaned as he hobbled back into a corner of the room to get the papers. "A pore way for the gov'ment to open up land, I says.

"Now down in the Oklahomy Run we used speed and brains to stake a claim, beating the other fellow to it. But it was a tough bunch down there, and sometimes, stranger, we—" he turned and pointed a gun straight at the man seated at the table, "we used a gun."

The old man who had stood leaning on his cane at the Drawing, complaining that neither legs nor brains counted in winning a claim, used his ingenuity to hold one.

During those last days of settling, Ida Mary and I lived in a state of tension and suspense. We watched our land plat and often rode out over the prairie to watch for the arrival of settlers whose land was being spotted. After a few of our deceptions, the claim jumpers became wary of the newspaper and cursed "that snip of a newspaper woman." And the girl who ran the post office was a government employee.

Here was a job for *The Wand*. In the next issue there appeared a black-headline article. It began:

"It has been reported that owing to the swift settlement of the Brulé, Secret Service Agents from the Federal Land Department are being sent out to protect the settlers against claim jumpers who are said to be nesting there. This tampering with government lands is a criminal offense, and it is understood that legal action will be pushed against all offenders."

One afternoon some two weeks later there walked into the print shop a man with an official manner about him. He called for the publisher of the paper.

"What do you know about this?" he demanded, pointing to the article. "What authority did you have for it?"

I was speechless. He was a Federal Agent.

"Well," I said at last, defiantly, "if the government is not furnishing agents on the land to look after these things, it should."

And it did. The agent looked into the matter, claim-jumping quieted down, there were fewer "spotters" swarming around, and soon, when their six months of grace had expired, the Lucky Numbers were all on the ground.

VIII. EASY AS FALLING
OFF A LOG

"Any old cayuse can enter a race," Bronco Benny remarked one day. "It's coming in under the wire that counts."

Ida Mary and I had saddled ourselves with a newspaper, a post office, a grocery store, an Indian trading post, and all the heavy labor of hauling, delivery of mail and odd jobs that were entailed. We were appalled to realize the weight of the responsibility we had assumed, with every job making steady, daily demands on us, with the Ammons finances to be juggled and stretched to cover constant demands on them. And there was no turning back.

The Lucky Numbers were all settled on their claims. Already trails were broken to the print shop from every direction. There was no time to plan, no time in which to wonder how one was to get things done. The important thing was to keep doing them. On the whole Strip there was not a vacant quarter-section. Already a long beaten trail led past the print-shop door north and south from Pierre to Presho; another crossed the reservation east and west from McClure to the Indian tepees and the rangeland beyond. Paths led in from all parts of the Strip like spokes, with Ammons the hub around which the wheel of the reservation's activities revolved.

From every section of the settlement the people gravitated to my claim; they came with their needs, with their plans, with their questions. In the first days we heard their needs rather than filled them, and the store and print shop became a place for the exchange of ideas and news, so that I was able to distinguish before long between the needs of the individual and those which were common to all, to clarify in my own mind the problems that beset the settlers as a whole, and to learn how some among them solved these problems.

Subscriptions for *The Wand* came in from the outside world, from people who had friends homesteading on the Brulé, and from people interested in the growth of the West. We had almost a thousand subscriptions at a dollar a year, and the money went into a team, equipment, and operation expenses. Ma Wagor helped in the store— she liked the "confusement," she said. She loved having people around her, and her curiosity about them all was insatiable. Ida or I generally made the mail trip.

The heavy labor we hired done when we could, but many times we hitched the team to the big lumber wagon and drove to Presho to bring out our own load of goods, including barrels of coal-oil and gasoline for automobiles, for there were quite a few cars on the reservation. Automobiles, in fact, were the only modern convenience in the lives of these modern pioneers who stepped from the running board straight back into the conditions of covered-wagon days.

The needs of the people were tremendous and insistent. And the needs of the people had to find expression in some way if they were to be met. The print shop was ready, *The Wand* was ready, I was ready— the only hitch was that I couldn't operate the new press we had bought, because we couldn't put it together. Ida Mary and I labored futilely with bolts and screws and other iron parts for two days.

I had sat down in the doorway to rest, exhausted by my tussle with the machinery, when I saw a man coming from the Indian settlement. He appeared against the horizon as if he had ridden out of the ether, riding slowly, straight as an Indian, but as he came closer I saw he was a white man. At the door he dismounted, threw the reins on the ground, and walked past me into the store, lifting his slouch hat as he entered. A man rather short of stature, sturdy, with a wide-set jaw and flat features that would have been homely had they not been so strong.

He looked with surprise through the open door of the print shop with its stalled machinery.

"What's the trouble?" he asked.

I explained my predicament. "I can't put the thing together and I don't know what to do about it. It would be almost impossible to get an experienced printer out here to start it for me."

He smiled broadly, walked into the shop, and without a word fixed the forms, adjusted the press and turned out the first issue of that strange-fated newspaper.

He would accept no pay and no thanks. "My name is Farraday, Fred Farraday," he said. "I'll ride over next Friday and help you get the paper out."

With that he mounted his blue-roan pony and rode away as deliberately as he had come. Every Friday after that he returned to help print the paper. Naturally we were curious about the man who had solved our desperate need for a printer in so surprising a way, but Fred was content to come week after week and disappear again on the horizon without any explanation as to who he was, where he came from, where he went when he rode out of sight each Friday.

We tried him with hints, with bland suppositions, with bare-faced questions, and could not break through his taciturnity. But even Fred had no defense against Ma Wagor's curiosity, and little by little, through her persistent questioning, we learned that he had a homestead near the Agency, that he had run a newspaper in the Northwest, and that he had been connected with the Indian Service.

The business of the newspaper increased rapidly, and advertising began to come in from the small surrounding towns. Ma Wagor was kept busy in the store, selling groceries to the Indians who camped around for a day dickering, and to the white settlers who were generally in a hurry. So little time! So much to do! Ida Mary helped me in the print shop, and before long we found we needed an expert typesetter. And I found one—unlikely as it may seem—on an adjoining claim. Kathryn Slattery, tall and slim and red-haired, preferred setting type to sitting alone in her shack, and with her striking appearance as an added attraction the popularity of the settlement with the young men homesteaders mounted.

In this odd fashion I found on the prairie both a printer and a typesetter, and for problems of format for *The Wand* there was always the cartoonist from Milwaukee. Late one afternoon I spied a strange, moving object in the far distance, something that bobbed up and down with the regularity of a clock pendulum. I asked Ida Mary in some bewilderment whether she could identify it. At last we saw it was a stiff-jointed quadruped with some sort of jumping-jack on top, bouncing up and down at every step. As it drew closer, heading for the shop, Ida Mary began to laugh. "It's Alexander Van Leshout," she said.

The cartoonist scrambled down from his mount and led the old, stiff-jointed, sway-backed horse up to the door. "I would have called sooner," he explained, sweeping off his hat in a low bow, "but I have been breaking in my new steed. Let me introduce Hop-Along Cassidy."

It was the newspaper that had brought him, he went on to say. "Editorially it's not so bad, but the make-up would give anyone sore eyes." It was Van Leshout who helped with the make-up of the paper, and he made drawings and had plates made that would do credit to any newspaper.

He was a strange character in this setting, like an exotic plant in an old-fashioned garden, and his eccentricities aroused considerable amusement among the settlers, although he became in time a favorite with them, serving as a sort of counter-irritant to the strain of pioneer life. Men who trudged all day through the broiling sun turning furrows in that stubborn soil were entertained by the strange antics of a man who sat before his cabin in the shade (when there was any) painting the Indians. It was a rare treat to hear him go on, they admitted, but he was not to be taken seriously.

Among the subscriptions I received for *The Wand* was one from the New York broker, Halbert Donovan, with a letter addressed to McClure.

"Through the McClure *Press* which I had sent me," it read, "I learned that you are running a newspaper out on some Indian reservation. I remember quite well the fantastic idea you had about doing things out there with a little newspaper. But it does not seem possible you would be so foolhardy.

"I'm afraid your aspirations are going to receive a great blow. It is a poor place for dreams. Imagine your trying to be a voice of the frontier, as you put it, to a bunch of homesteaders in a God-forsaken country like that. If I can be of help to you in some way, you might let me know. You have shown a progressive spirit. Too bad to waste it."

What I needed at the moment was to have him send me a few corporations, but as that was unlikely, I pinned my faith in *The Wand*. It was a seven-column, four-page paper which carried staunchly a strange load of problems and responsibilities. In spite of the New York broker's blunt disbelief in the possibilities of a frontier newspaper, I had become more and more convinced during those weeks that only through some such medium could the homesteaders express their own needs, in their own way; have their problems discussed in terms of their own immediate situation.

We needed herd laws and a hundred other laws; we needed new land rulings. We needed schools, bridges across draws and dry creeks. We needed roads. In fact, there was nothing which we did not need—and most of all we needed a sense of close-knit cooperation. Aside from these matters of general interest, relating to their common welfare, the paper attempted to acquaint the settlers with one another, to inform them of the activities going on about them, to keep them advised of frontier conditions. To assist those who knew nothing of farming conditions in the West, and often enough those who had never farmed before, I reprinted articles on western soil and crops, and on the conservation of moisture.

Every week there were noticeable strides in that incredible country toward civilization, changes and improvements. These were printed as quickly as I learned of them, not only because of the encouragement this record of tangible results might bring the homesteaders, but also as a means of information for people in the East who still did not know what we were doing and who did not see the possibilities of the land.

And already, in depicting the homestead movement, I had begun to realize that the Lower Brulé was only a fraction of what was to come, and I reached out in panoramic scope to other parts of the frontier.

And already, though but dimly, I had begun to see that the system of cooperation which was being attempted—cautiously and on a small scale—was the logical solution for the farmer's problems, not alone in this homesteading area, not alone on the Lower Brulé; but that like a pebble thrown into a quiet stream it must make ever-widening circles until it encompassed the farmers throughout the West, perhaps—

Naturally public issues sprang up which neither Ida Mary nor I knew how to handle. We knew nothing about politics, nothing at all about the proper way to go about setting things right. But we were a jump ahead of the Lower Brulé settlers in homesteading experience, and there were many local issues with which to make a start.

One of the first public issues the paper took up was an attack on the railroad company in regard to the old bridge spanning the Missouri River at Chamberlain. "Every time a shower comes up, that bridge goes out," declared *The Wand*, and it wasn't much of an exaggeration. The homesteaders were dependent on the bridge to get immigrant goods across, and with the heavy rains that season many settlers had been delayed in getting on their land or in getting their crops planted in time.

The Wand referred to the railroad report that this was the biggest immigration period of the state's history, with 537 carloads of immigrant goods moved in during the first twelve days of the month. For several years the small towns west of the Missouri had been making a fight for a new bridge. "The Lower Brulé settlers want a new bridge," I wrote. "And if the Milwaukee does not build one we are going to do our shipping over the Northwestern regardless of longer hauls." I had not talked this matter over with the settlers, but they would do it, all right.

A flea attacking an elephant! But a flea can be annoying, and we would keep it up. I was encouraged when civic leaders of several small towns sent for copies of the article to use in their petitions to the company. It was the voice of the Lower Brulé, and already the Lower Brulé bore weight.

In practical ways the paper also tried to serve the homesteaders, keeping them posted on other frontier regions and the methods employed there to bring the land into production. It made a study of crops best adapted to the frontier; it became the Strip's bureau of information and a medium of exchange—not only of ideas but of commodities.

In new country, where money is scarce, people resort from necessity to the primitive method of barter, exchanging food for fuel, labor for commodities. There is a good deal to be said in its favor, and it solved a lot of problems in those early, penniless days.

We had started the post office mainly as a means of getting the newspaper into circulation, and it had developed into a difficult business of its own which required more and more of Ida Mary's time. Friday was publication day. On Thursday we printed the paper so as to have it ready for Friday's mail, and on Thursday night the tin reflectors of the print-shop lamps threw their lights out for miles across the prairie far into the night, telling a lost people the day of the week. "It's Thursday night—the night the paper goes to press," more than one homesteader said as he saw it.

It was a long, tedious job to print so many newspapers on a hand press one at a time, fold and address them. It took the whole Ammons force and a few of the neighbors to get it ready for the mail, which must meet the McClure mail stage at noon. While one of us rushed off with the mail, others at home would address the local list of papers and put them in the mail boxes by the time the return mail came in for distribution.

Our U. S. mail transport was our old topless One-Hoss Shay—repaired and repainted for the purpose—with the brown team hitched to it. It was a long, hot drive, eight miles, to meet the stage, which reached McClure at noon, jolting along under a big cotton umbrella wired to the back of the seat for shade. I slapped the brown team with the lines and consoled myself that if roughing it put new life into one's body I should be good for a hundred years.

When we were behind time and the mail was light or there was money going out, we ran Lakota through as a pony express. Lakota was a gift from the Indians, whose name meant "banded together as friends." One day Running Deer had come over to Ammons, leading a little bronc. He had caught her in a bunch of wild horses which roamed the plains, a great white stallion at their head. "One day—two day—three day—I have made run, so swift like eagle. Then I rope her and make broke for ride."

She was a beauty. Graceful, proud—and lawless. "Good blood, like Indian chief," said Running Deer with pride in this gift from the Sioux. "But white squaw—she throw um, mebbe. Rub like fawn—" and he stroked her curved neck.

There was no "mebbe" about throw um white squaw. One had to be on the lookout or "swift like eagle" she would jump from under one at the slightest provocation. But we trained her to carry the mail, and though there was no banditry in that section, we had to be on our guard with money coming in. No man would ever grab the mail sack from Lakota's back. That little outlaw would paw him to death.

Whether we caught the mail stage or not often depended upon the mood of the stage driver. If he felt tired and lazy he patiently sat in front of the Halfway House at McClure and "chawed" and spat until he saw the Ammons mail coming over the trail. If he were out of sorts he drove on.

All we got out of the post-office job was the cancellation of stamps, as it was a fourth-class office in which the government furnished the stamps and we kept the money for all stamps canceled in our office. But the settlers were too busy to write letters, so the income

87

was small and the incoming mail, for which we received no pay, weighed us down with work. For months after the settlers came west they ordered many commodities by mail, and their friends sent them everything from postcards to homemade cookies and jelly, so as mail carriers we became pack mules. But we went on carrying mail. It is easier to get into things than to get out.

Much of the ordering of commodities by the settlers was done through the huge mail-order catalogs issued by half a dozen large companies in the East. Those mail-order catalogs were of enormous importance to the homesteaders. For the women they had the interest of a vast department store through which one could wander at will. In a country where possessions were few and limited to essentials, those pages with their intriguing cuts represented most of the highly desirable things in life.

From the mail-order catalogs they ordered their stoves, most of their farming implements, and later, when the contrast between the alluring advertisements and the bleak shacks grew too strong for the women to endure, fancy lamps for the table, and inexpensive odds and ends which began to transform those rough barren houses into livable homes.

Running a newspaper out here was, as Ma Wagor had predicted, a "pestiferous" job. One day we hung the rubber roller out to dry and the sun melted it flat. As a result Ada had to ride to McClure to borrow one from *The Press* before we could print the paper. There was no way to get the ready-prints without making the long trip to Presho. Finally every homesteader around Ammons who went to town stopped in at the express office to get them for us. It was a multiplication of effort but we generally got the prints.

But, hard as it was, the work did not tire me as much as the mere mechanical grind of the hammer-and-tongs work on *The Press* had done. Each day was so filled with new problems and new interests, so crammed with activity, that we were carried along by the exhilaration of it. One cannot watch an empire shoot up around him like Jack's beanstalk without feeling the compulsion to be a part of that movement, that growth. And the worst barrier we had to face had vanished—the initial prejudice against two young girls attempting to take an active part in the forward movement of the community.

The obstacles of a raw country had no effect on Ada Long, our fourteen-year-old helper. She came of a struggling family who had settled on an alkali claim set back from everything until the Brulé settlers had broken a trail past it. So Ada, finding herself in a new moving world, was happy. With her long yellow braids hanging beneath a man's straw hat, strong capable hands, and an easy stride, she went about singing hymns as she worked, taking upon herself many tasks that she was not called upon to perform. And Fred Farraday was taking much of the heavy work of the print shop off our hands.

Ma Wagor, too, was an invaluable help to us. "All my life I've wanted to run a store," she admitted. "I like the confusement." Every morning she came across the prairie sitting straight as a board in the old buggy behind a spotted horse that held his head high and his neck stretched like a giraffe. The few dollars she got for helping in the store eked out Pa's small pension, which had been their only revenue.

The commodities handled at the store had increased from coffee and matches to innumerable supplies. The faithful team, Fan and Bill, were kept on the road most of the time. We made business trips to Presho and Pierre. Help was not always available, and there could be no waste movements in a wasteland. On some of these trips we hitched the team to the big lumber wagon and hauled out barrels of oil, flour, printers' ink and other supplies for all and sundry of our enterprises. It had come to that.

"There go the Ammons sisters," people would say as the wagon started, barrels rattling, down the little main street of Presho, off to the hard trail home.

Slim and straight and absurdly small, in trim shirt waists, big sombreros tilted over our heads, we bounced along on the wagon, trying to look as mature and dignified as our position of business women demanded.

"Those are the two Brulé girls who launched an attack on the Milwaukee railroad," Presho people remarked. "Well, I'll be damned!"

Once when I was too ill to leave Presho and we stayed for the night in a little frame hotel, Doc Newman came in to look me over.

"Do you girls get enough nourishing food?" he asked.

"We eat up all the store profits," lamented Ida Mary.

He laughed. "Keep on eating them up. And slow down."

Pioneer women, old and new, went through many hardships and privations. The sodbreakers' women over the Strip worked hard, but their greatest strain was that of endurance rather than heavy labor. But refreshing nights with the plains at rest and exhilarating morning air were the restoratives.

Hard and unrelieved as their lives were in many respects, gallantly as they shouldered their part of the burden of homesteading, the women inevitably brought one important factor into the homesteaders' lives. They inaugurated some form of social life, and with the exchange of visits, the impromptu parties, the informal gatherings, and the politeness, the amenities they demanded—however modified to meet frontier conditions—civilization came to stay.

The instinct of women to build up the forms of social life is deeprooted and historically sound. Out of the forms grow traditions, and from the traditions grow permanency, which is woman's only protection. With the first conscious development of social life on the Brulé, the Strip took on a more settled air.

Meanwhile, out of the back-breaking labor the first results began to appear. The sodbreakers were going to have a crop. And hay—hay to feed their livestock and to sell. Everyone passing through the Strip stopped to look at the many small fields and a few large ones dotting the prairie. People came from other parts of the frontier to see the rapid development which the Brulé had made.

"Mein Gott in Himmel!" shouted old Mr. Husmann, pointing to a field of oats. "Look at them oats. We get one hell of a crop for raw land."

On the other side of us, Chris Christopherson's big field of flax was in full bloom, like a blue flower garden.

"I come by Ioway," Mr. Husmann went on, "when she was a raw country, and I say, 'Mein Gott, what grass!' But I see no grass so high and rich like this."

The gardens matured late, as all growth on the western prairie does. The seed which was sown on the sod so unusually late that year never would have come up but for the soaking rains. Now there were lettuce, radishes, onions and other things. One could not buy fresh green vegetables anywhere in the homestead country, and they were like manna from Heaven. It had been almost a year since Ida Mary and I had tasted green foods. It is a curious paradox that people living on the land depended for food or canned goods from the cities, and that the fresh milk and cream and green vegetables associated with farm life were unattainable.

Most of the settlers lived principally on beans and potatoes with some dried fruits, but we had bought canned fruits, oranges and apples, pretending to ourselves that we would stock them for the store. Some of the settlers could buy such foods in small quantities, for they had a little money that first summer; but the Indians were our main customers for the more expensive things, buying anything we wanted to sell them when they got their government allowances. While their money lasted they had no sales resistance whatever.

This characteristic apparently wasn't peculiar to the Brulé Indians, but was equally true of those in the Oklahoma reservation who boomed the luxury trades when oil was discovered on their land. There it was no uncommon sight to see a gaudy limousine parked outside a tepee and a grand piano on the ground inside.

But what the Indians didn't buy of these foods at forbidden costs we ate ourselves, cutting seriously into our profits. And when Mrs. Christopherson sent her little Heine over one day with a bucket of green beans we almost foundered as animals do with the first taste of green feed after a winter of dry hay.

We had a few rows of garden east of our shack. I remember gathering something out of it—lettuce and onions, probably, which grew abundantly without any care.

It was hot, and everybody on the Strip, worn out from strenuous weeks, slowed down. The plains were covered with roses, wild roses trying to push their heads above the tall grass. The people who had worked so frantically, building houses, putting in crops, walked more slowly now, stopped to talk and rest a little, and sit in the shade. They discovered how tired they were, and the devitalizing heat added to the general torpor.

"It's this confusement," Ma Wagor said, "that's wore everybody out." She was the only one on the Strip to continue at the same energetic pace. "There ain't a bit of use wearing yourself out, trying to do the things here the Almighty Himself hasn't got around to yet—flying right in the face of the Lord, I says to myself sometimes."

But in spite of the heat and the general weariness, the work was unrelenting. The mail must be delivered regularly. The paper must be printed. One day Ida Mary's voice burst in upon the clicking of type.

"What are we going to do about the rattlesnakes?" she said tragically; "they're taking the country."

She was right. They were taking the reservation. They wriggled through the tall grass making ribbon waves as they went. They coiled like a rubber hose along the trails, crawled up to the very doors, stopped there only by right-fitting screens.

One never picked up an object without first investigating with a board or stick lest there be a snake under it. It became such an obsession that if anyone did pick up something without finding a snake under it he felt as disappointed as if he had run to a fire and found it out when he got there.

On horseback or afoot one was constantly on the lookout for them. For those gray coiled horrors were deadly. We knew that. There were plenty of stories of people who heard that dry rattle, saw the lightning speed of the strike and the telltale pricks on arm or ankle, and waited for the inevitable agony and swift death. The snakes always sounded their warning, the chilling rattle before they struck, but they rarely gave time for escape.

Sourdough stopped at the store one morning for tobacco. He had a pair of boots tied to his saddle and when Ida Mary stepped to the door to hand him the tobacco, a rattlesnake slithered out from one of the boots. He jumped off his horse and killed it.

"Damn my skin," Sourdough exclaimed, "and here I slept on them boots last night for a pillow. I oughta stretched a rope."

Plainsmen camping out made it a practice to stretch a rope around camp or pallet as a barricade against snakes; they would not cross the hairy, fuzzy rope, we were told. It may be true, but there was not a rope made that I would trust to keep snakes out on that reservation.

I remember camping out one night with a group of homesteaders. The ground was carefully searched and a rope stretched before we turned in, but it was a haggard, white-faced group which started back the next morning. True, there hadn't been any rattlesnakes, but from the amount of thinking about them that had been done that night, there might as well have been.

A young homesteader rushed into the print shop one day, white as a sheet. "A snake," he gasped, "a big rattler across the trail in front of the store."

"What of it? Haven't you ever seen a snake before?"

"Have I!" he replied dismally. "I saw them for six months back there in Cleveland. But my snakes didn't rattle."

Ours rattled. The rattle of the snake became as familiar as the song of the bird. The settlers were losing livestock every day. Everyone was in danger. With the hot dry weather they became bigger and thicker. The cutting of great tracts of grass for hay stirred them into viperous action. They were harder to combat than droughts and blizzards. Not many regions were so thickly infested as that reservation. Those snakes are a part of its history.

"Couldn't be many in other regions," Olaf Rasmusson, an earnest young farmer, said dryly; "they're all settled here."

"Look out for snakes!" became the watchword on the Strip.

Mrs. Christopherson's little Heine, a small, taciturn boy of five who had become a daily, silent visitor at the store, came in one afternoon, roused into what, for him, was a garrulous outburst:

"There's a snake right out here, and I bet it's six feet long the way it rattles."

Ada grabbed a pole and tried to kill it. The monster struck back like the cracking of a whip. She backed off and with her strong arm hit again and again, while Ida Mary ran with a pitchfork.

"Keep out of the way," shouted Ada, "you may get bitten!"

Winded, Ada fanned herself with her straw hat and wiped the perspiration from her face. "I got that fellow," she said triumphantly.

This was one problem about which *The Wand* seemed helpless. Printers' ink would have no effect on the snakes, and if this horror were published, the Strip would be isolated like a leper's colony. After using so much ingenuity in building up the achievements of that swift-growing country, the announcement of this plague of snakes might undo all that had been accomplished.

And the snakes increased. When Ida Mary was out of sight I worried constantly. It was like one's fear for a person in battle, who may be struck by a bullet at any moment. But the rattler was more surely fatal when it struck than the bullet.

Something had to be done. To Hades with what the world thought about our having snakes! We had to do something that would bring relief from this horror. We went to the old medicine men—John Yellow Grass, I think was one of them—to find out how the Indians got rid of snakes. They didn't. But at least they knew what to do when you had been bitten. The Indian medicine men said to bleed the wound instantly, bandaging the flesh tightly above and below to keep the poison from circulating. That was the Indians' first-aid treatment; and, as a last resort, "suck the wound."

The Wand printed warnings: "Bank your houses ... keep doors and windows tightly screened ... keep a bottle of whisky close at hand.... Carry vinegar, soda and bandages with you, and a sharp thin-bladed knife to slash and bleed the wound." What a run there was on vinegar and pocket knives!

By this time the sight of a coiled rope made me jumpy and I dreamed of snakes writhing, coiling, moving in undulating lines. At noon one day I was alone, making up the paper. I stood at the form table working, when I turned abruptly. A snake's slimy head was thrust through a big knothole in the floor. Its beady eyes held me for a moment, as they are said to hypnotize a bird. I could neither move nor scream.

Then with a reflex action I threw an empty galley—an oblong metal tray used to put the set type in—square over the hole. The snake moved so quickly it missed the blow and lay under the floor hissing like an engine letting off steam. It would have been in the print shop in another second. The floor was laid on 2 × 4 inch scantlings, so there was nothing to keep snakes from working their way under. It should have been banked around the foundation with sod.

The next day a homesteader's little girl was bitten. Oh, for serum! But if there were any such life-saver on the market we had no way of getting it.

The Wand called a meeting of the settlers and laid plans of warfare against the snakes. The homesteaders organized small posses. And cowboys and Indian bucks joined in that war against the reptiles.

They killed them by the dozens in every conceivable manner. The cowboys were always telling about shooting their heads off, and they said the Indians used an arrow, spearing them in the neck just back of the head. They never let one get away if they could help it. Some of them claimed they picked up rattlesnakes by the tails and cracked their heads off.

The snakes wintered in the prairie-dog holes, but I never heard of a prairie dog being bitten by one of them. On warm days in late fall the snakes came out of the holes and lay coiled thick on the ground, sunning themselves, while the little dogs sat up on their hind legs and yipped in their squeaky voices. The settlers and cowboys invaded the dog towns and killed off the snakes by the hundred. Dog towns were the tracts where the prairie dogs made their homes. During the intensive snake war, a homesteader came from one of the big prairie-dog towns to take us over to look at the kill.

There, strung on wires, hung more than a hundred huge, horrid rattlers, many of them still wriggling and twisting and coiling like a thrown lariat.

It seems too bad the snakeskin industry of today missed that bonanza of supply, and that science did not make a more general use of rattlesnake serum at that time. The settlers would have made some easy money and science would have got serum in unlimited quantity.

This is a gruesome subject. The constant, lurking menace of the snakes was one of the hardest things the frontier had to endure, harder than drought or blizzard, but in one way and another we came through.

Instead of *The Wand's* campaign against snakes injuring the Strip it created a great deal of interest, and people said we were "subduing the frontier."

Easy? Oh, yes; easy as falling off a log.

IX. THE OPENING OF THE ROSEBUD

The settling of those western lands was as elemental as the earth, and no phase of its settlement was as dramatic as the opening of the Rosebud. Homesteading was now the biggest movement in America. We were entering a great period of land development running its course between 1909 and our entrance into the World War in 1917. The people were land crazy. The western fever became an epidemic that spread like a prairie fire. Day by day we watched the vast, voluntary migration of a people.

Men with families to support, frail women with no one to help them, few of them with money enough to carry them through, took the chance, with the odds against them. I have seen men appear with their families, ten dollars in their pockets, or only five after the filing fee on the land was paid. I have seen them sleep on the prairie, get odd jobs here and there until they could throw up a shelter out of scrap lumber, and slowly get a foothold, often becoming substantial citizens of a community they helped to build.

Free land! Free land! It was like the tune piped by the Pied Piper. "This is the chance for the poor man," I wrote in *The Wand*. "When the supply of free land is exhausted the poor man cannot hope to own land.... If the moneyed powers get hold of this cheap land as an investment, they will force the price beyond the grasp of the masses.... The West is the reserve upon which the future growth and food supply of the nation must depend."

Ida Mary said that I was running to land as a Missourian did to mules, but *The Wand* was fast becoming identified with the land movement.

As the homesteaders flowed in a great sea out of the towns and cities into the West, one wondered at their courage. There was not the hope which inspires a gold rush, the possibility of a gold strike which may bring sudden wealth and ease. The road was long, the only likely signs of achievement an extra room on the shack, a few more acres of ground turned under. And—eventual security! That was it, security. A piece of ground that belonged to them, on which they could plant their feet, permanency.

In answer to that cry for land there came another proclamation from the President, Theodore Roosevelt. Another great tract of land, the great Rosebud Indian Reservation, with a million acres of homesteads, was to be thrown open. A lottery with 1500 square miles of territory as the sweepstakes and 100,000 people playing its wheel of fortune. Trying to describe its size and sweep and significance, I find myself, in the vernacular of the range, plumb flabbergasted.

Of course, there were some among the homesteaders on the Lower Brulé who found the grass greener on the Rosebud, and wanted to throw up their claims and move on to new ground; but the government informed them, somewhat grimly, that they could prove up where they were, or not at all. And I can understand their restlessness. To this day I never hear of some new frontier being developed without pricking up my ears and quivering like a circus horse when he hears a band play. There are some desert products that can't be rooted out—sagebrush and cactus and the hold of the open spaces.

The Rosebud Opening was one of the most famous lotteries of them all. The Rosebud reservation lay in Tripp County, across White River from the Brulé. Its conversion into homesteads meant an immediate income for the United States Treasury, but according to a recent law, all monies received from the sale of the lands were to be deposited to the credit of the Indians belonging to and having tribal rights on the reservation, the funds thus acquired to be used by Congress for the education, support and civilization of the Indians.

The name Rosebud was emblazoned across the nation, after the government proclamation, in the newspapers, in railroad pamphlets, on public buildings. As usual, the railroads played a major part in aiding prospective settlers to reach the registration points, a half-dozen little western villages.

The frontier town of Pierre had been unprepared for the avalanche of people who had descended upon it during the Lower Brulé opening. Service and equipment had been inadequate. In the great Bonesteel Opening a few years earlier, gambling and lawlessness had run riot. Therefore Superintendent Witten formulated and revised the drawing system, endeavoring to work out the most suitable plan for disposing of these tracts so that there might be no suggestion of unfairness.

Railroads traversing the West had already begun to extend their lines still farther into the little-populated section, starting new towns along their lines, running landseekers' excursions in an effort to show the people what this country had to offer them.

In preparation for the Rosebud Opening they prepared for the influx of people on a gigantic scale, made ready to take whole colonies from various sections of the East and Middle West to the reservation.

Among the registration points was the little town of Presho. A crude, unfinished little town, with a Wild West flavor about it, Presho couldn't help doing things in a spectacular fashion. Like most hurriedly built frontier towns, there was little symmetry to it—two irregular rows of small business places, most of them one-story structures, with other shops and offices set back on side streets. Its houses were set hit-and-miss, thickly dotting the prairie around its main street. Two years before, it had been merely an unsettled stretch of prairie.

Then the Milwaukee railroad platted the town, bringing out carloads of people to the auction. Two men, named Dirks and Sedgwick, paid $500 for the first lot, on which to start a bank. That was $480 more than the list price.

97

They had a little building like a sheep wagon, or a cook shack, on wheels, which they rolled onto the lot. Within eight minutes the bank was open for business. The first deposit, in fact, was made while the sheep-wagon bank rolled along. Two barrels and a plank served as a counter.

The two founders had the necessary $5000 capital, and when the cashier went to dinner he took all the money with him, with two six-shooters for protection. He was never robbed. For two years, during the land boom, the bank had not closed, day or night.

Locators coming in, in the middle of the night, from their long trips over the territory, would knock on the door in the back end of the bank. The banker would open the door a crack, stick his gun out and demand, "Who's there?"

"It's Kimball. Got a bunch of seekers here. They have to catch the train east."

The locator or other person wanting to transact business after the banker had gone to bed had to identify himself before the door was opened. When the homestead movement of that region was at its height, thousands of dollars passed over the board-and-barrel counter in the bank's night-time business.

"The Rosebud has been throwed open!" went the cry. The entire western country made ready for the invasion of the landseekers. The government red tape for the lottery, with its various registration points, would require a small army to handle. It was one of the most gigantic governmental programs ever known. Notaries had to be appointed to take care of the affidavits, land locators selected to show the seekers the land, accommodations provided for the 115,000 who registered in that Drawing.

Even the Brulé was crowded with people ready to play their luck in the land lottery. Every available corner was utilized for sleeping space, and the store at Ammons did a record business that would help pay the wholesale bills at Martin's store. Ida Mary was busy taking care of postal duties, handling increased mail, government notices, etc.

During the summer our financial condition had gone from bad to worse.

"Do you know those Ammons girls?" one native westerner asked another. "Came out from St. Louis, about as big as my Annie (Annie was about twelve); head wranglers out on the Lower Brulé, newspaper, trading post, whole works."

"Well, they'll last till their money is gone."

And it was about gone! "What are we going to do to meet these payments, Edith?" Ida Mary asked one day in a breathing spell. There wasn't enough money to pay for groceries, printing equipment, interest, etc.

If we could only hold on, the proof notices would bring in $2000 or more, which was big money out there. But the proof season was almost a year ahead, and the money had already been pledged.

Profit and loss! My head ached. I felt as though I had been hit on the head by 200 square miles of Brulé sod. Ma Wagor offered us a way out of one of our difficulties. She'd always wanted a store. She liked the "confusement." So we turned the store over to the Wagors', lock, stock and barrel—prunes and molasses, barrels of coal-oil and vinegar, padlocks on the doors. They had no money, but Ma wanted it as much as we wanted to be rid of it, so it was a satisfactory deal. They were to pay us on a percentage basis. We still had a claim, a post office and a newspaper to manage, and the Indian trade to handle.

"It looks as though the Ammons venture is going under," people were beginning to say. I went to Presho and the small towns near by, and, somewhat to my own surprise, succeeded in getting more advertising for *The Wand*. But it wasn't enough.

One night I came home, determined that something must be done. The whole arrangement seemed to me unfair to Ida Mary. "Sister," I said, "I'm going to give up the claim."

She quietly put down her book, open so as not to lose the page, and waited for me to go on.

"I told Mr. West today that we would sell. I am going to pay off the mortgage on your homestead, clean up the other debts, and—"

"And then what?"

"I don't know."

"Don't give up your land, Edith. Something will happen. Something always happens." She went back to her book.

Something did happen. The Rosebud Opening. I was to cover it for a western newspaper syndicate, and this time I had the inside track. Being familiar with the field and with the government lottery operations, I would be able to get my stories out while other reporters were finding out what it was all about.

Remembering the money I had made with the little verses printed on a postcard at the Brulé Opening, I prepared another on the Rosebud, with the cartoonist from Milwaukee helping me by making drawings to illustrate it. Then, armed with the postcards, I set off for Presho—and the Rosebud.

On a Sunday night in early October, 1908, I stood on a corner of the dark main street of Presho waiting for the Rosebud to open. I had appointed agents to handle my postcards and I was free to cover the story. Special trains loaded with landseekers were coming. The confusion of last-minute preparations to receive them was at its height.

I found Presho as mad as a hornet. The Milwaukee railroad had taken the turntable out, and special trains coming in from Chicago and other points east must thus go on to the next town to turn around. This was bound to cut into Presho's share of the crowds. As long as the town had been the turning point of the road, it was one of the greatest trade centers in that part of the West.

The lottery was to start Monday, which meant the stroke of midnight. The little town was ready, its dark streets lighted here and there by flaring arc lights. Up and down Main Street, and out over the fields, tents had been erected to take care of the crowd.

And the trains were coming in, unloading their human cargo. Others poured in by every conceivable means of transportation, invading the little frontier town, the only spot of civilization in the vast, bare stretch of plains. Presho woke to find a great drove of tenderfeet stampeding down its little Main Street. They thundered down the board sidewalk and milled in the middle of the road, kicking up dust like a herd of range cattle as they went.

Aside from the great tents put up by some of the towns for lodging and eating quarters, small tents dotted the outskirts. People were bringing their own camping equipment, and I might add that only those who had such foresight, slept during those turbulent days.

The daily train was an event in these frontier towns, its coming watched by most of the inhabitants. Now five and six a day roared in, spilled 500 to 800 passengers into the packed streets, and roared away again. As the heavily loaded trains met or passed each other along the route the excited crowds called jovially to one another, "Suckers! Suckers!" With but 4000 claims, the chance to win was slim.

On the station platform, in the thick of the crowds, were the Indians. After all, it appeared, they were learning from the white man. This time they had come in an enlightened and wholly commercial spirit. Brave in paint and feathers and beads, they strolled about, posing for the landseekers—for 50 cents a picture.

A maze of last-minute activity was under way before the stroke of midnight. Telephone companies installed additional equipment and service. Telegraph wires were being strung up. Expert men were being rushed out from Kansas City and Omaha to take care of the flood of words that would soon go pouring out to the nation—telling the story of the gamble for land.

A magazine editor, notebook in hand, moved from one group of seekers to another, asking: "Do you think Taft will be elected?" He didn't seem to be getting far. On the eve of a presidential election a people was turning to the soil for security. "Do you think Taft will be elected?" the editor repeated patiently. "Who gives a damn?" shouted a steel worker from Philadelphia.

A train lumbered in heavily from Chicago, fourteen coaches, crowded to standing room only, men and women herded and tagged like sheep. They stumbled out onto the dark platform, jostled among the mob already assembled, exhausted, dirty, half-asleep, yet shaking with excitement. That high-pitched excitement, of course, was partly due to strain and suspense, partly to the gambling spirit in which the lottery was carried out. But for the most part the crowd generated its own excitement through its great numbers and consequent rivalry, as it entered the dark streets with their glaring lights, the mad confusion of shouting and band playing.

They came from Chicago and jerkwater towns in Nebraska, from farms and steel mills, from the stage and the pulpit. School teachers and farm boys, clerks and stenographers, bookkeepers and mechanics, business men and lawyers. Perhaps the most significant thing was the presence of those business men, often coming in whole groups to study the country and its possibilities, to be on hand when the town sites were opened, to be the first to start businesses on the Rosebud.

On the Brulé there had been nothing but the land. Here the plows, the farm implements, salesmen of every conceivable commodity needed by settlers, were on hand. These people were to start with supplies in sight, with business organizing in advance to handle their problems, with capital waiting for their needs.

And they came by the thousands. From Chicago alone there came one group of 3000 seekers. "Move on," came the endless chant. "Move on!" It didn't matter where, so long as they kept moving, making way for new mobs of restless people. "Move on!"

Wires were clicking with news from the other registration points. Presho, to its fury, couldn't compare with some of the other towns. The little town of Dallas had gone stark mad. Thirty-four carloads of seekers were due in these villages between midnight and morning. They were coming from every direction, bringing, along with the individual seekers, whole groups of New England farmers, Iowa business men, an organization of clerks from Cleveland, and from everywhere the ruddy-faced farmers.

Over the uproar of the crowd could be heard the sharp staccato click of the telegraph wires. Special trains were coming from Omaha, came the news. The police force had tried to keep the crowds from smothering each other, but they had torn down the gate of the station and rushed through, afraid to be left behind.

Runners came overland across the empty Rosebud to carry the news from the little towns, riding hell-for-leather, their horses foaming although the night was cold. "You ought to see Dallas, folks! People lighting like grasshoppers.... You ought to see Gregory!" The rivalry was bitter among the towns, each trying to corner as much of the crowd as possible.

Presho was sending out word vehemently denying the reports that an epidemic of black smallpox had broken out there.

Men representing everything from flop tents to locating agents boarded trains en route, trying to persuade the seekers to register at their respective towns. And all of them were bitter against the railroads, which were furnishing return accommodations every few hours, giving the tradesmen little chance to make their fortunes, as many of them had confidently expected to do.

Automobiles, many bought for the occasion, lined the streets of these border towns, ready to take the seekers over the land—if they stayed long enough. It surprised the easterners, this evidence of modernity in a pioneer world. And here and there a new automobile parked beside a prairie schooner.

Curiously enough, the price of the land distributed by the Openings was higher than that of vast tracts of untouched land in the West which was also available to the public, and yet attention was concentrated solely on the Rosebud; the desire for land there was at fever heat, while other land was regarded with apathy. Whether this was due to the fact that the other land was little known, or to the madness that attends any gambling operation and the intensive advertising which had called attention to the Rosebud, I do not know.

But this land was not free. For these Indian lands the government charged from $2.00 to $6.00 an acre, according to classification. Thus 160 acres of first-class land would cost the homesteader around a thousand dollars—one-fifth down, the rest in annual payments under the five-year proof plan. If he made commutation proof in fourteen months, the minimum residence required, he must then make payment in full.

102

The hours wore on toward midnight and the crowd grew denser. "Move on," droned the chant. "Move on!" The editor had turned the page of his notebook and spoke to one of the women landseekers. "Are you a suffragette?" he asked politely. Pushing back an elbow that had grazed her cheek, pulling her hat firmly over her head, clutching her handbag firmly, she looked at him, wonderingly. "Are you—" he began again, but someone shouted "Move on," and the woman disappeared in the throng.

At the stroke of midnight a cry went up from the registrars. At 12:01 under the dim flicker of coal-oil lanterns and torches hung on posts or set on barrels and boxes, that most famous of lotteries began.

The uproar and confusion of the hours before midnight were like a desert calm compared with the clamor which broke out. Registrars lined both sides of the street. "Right this way, folks! Here you are, here you are! Register right here!" And there, on rough tables, on dry-goods boxes, anything upon which a piece of paper could be filled out and a notary seal stamped thereon, the crowd put in their applications as entries in the gamble, raised their right hands and swore: "I do solemnly swear that I honestly desire to enter public lands for my own personal use as a home and for settlement and cultivation, and not for speculation or in the interest of some other person...."

In the excitement and chill of the October night, fingers shook so that they could scarcely hold a pen. Commissioned notaries were getting 25 cents a head from the applicants. Real estate offices were jammed.

In between the registration stands were the hot-dog and coffee booths with the tenders yelling, while thick black coffee flowed into tin cups by the barrel, and sandwiches were handed out by the tubful. Popcorn and peanut venders pushed through the crowd crying their wares. And among the voices were those of the agents who were selling my postcards, selling them like liniment in a patent-medicine show.

Spielers shouted the virtues of the food or drink or tent or land locator they were advertising. Even the notaries got megaphones to announce their services—until government authorities stepped in and threatened to close them all up.

Into the slits in the huge cans which held the applications dropped a surprising number of items. People became confused and used it as a mail box, dropping in souvenir cards. One applicant even dropped in his return fare. And some, shaking uncontrollably with excitement, were barely able to drop their applications in at all.

And somewhere, off in the dark spaces beyond the flickering lights, lay the million acres of land for which the horde was clamoring, its quiet sleep unbroken.

There was a sharp tug at my arm, and I turned to see the reporter from Chicago who had filed on the Brulé Opening.

"I'm trying my luck again," he said.

So he had not won in the Brulé lottery. Somehow I was glad to know that was the reason for his not being on a claim there.

Sensing this, he said grimly: "So you thought I was a quitter."

As we clung to each other to keep from being separated in the hysterical mob, I heard his hollow cough.

"Are you ill?" I asked.

"It's this crowd and the dust—my lungs—got to come west—"

I grabbed him by the coat sleeve, trying to make my voice carry above the ballyhoo. "If you do not win here, come and see me. I can get you a claim." The swaying throng separated us.

I rushed to the telegraph office and sent off my story. As I started back I stopped to look upon the little town which had been started at the end of the iron trail, revealed in the light of torches against a black sky, and at the faces, white and drawn and tense.

Move on! Move on! At 4 o'clock that Monday morning, four hours after arrival, the landseekers who had registered were on the road back to Chicago and all points east, many of them carrying in one hand a chunk of sod and in the other a tuft of grass—tangible evidence that they had been on the land. And other trains were rushing out, carrying more people. I boarded a returning special which was packed like a freight train full of range cattle, men and women travel-stained, tired and hollow-eyed, but geared up by hope.

I got off at Chamberlain. The rumors had been correct. That seething mob at Presho was only the spray cast by the tidal wave. At Chamberlain long, heavily loaded trains pulled in and out. People walked ten and twelve abreast through the streets. Some 30,000 strangers besieged that frontier town. A mob of 10,000 tried to fill out application blanks, tried to get something to eat and drink, some place to sleep. While the saloons were overrun, there was little drunkenness. No man could stand at the bar long enough to get drunk. If he managed to get one drink, or two at most, he was pushed aside before he could get another—to make room for someone else. Move on! Move on!

The stockmen were shocked. They had not dreamed of anything like this invasion. Their range was going and they owned none, or little, of the land. The old Indians looked on, silent and morose.

Hotels, locating agents, all the First Chance and Last Chance saloons became voluntary distributors of my postcards. It looked as though I too were going to reap a harvest from the Rosebud Opening.

And they continued to come! Within four days 60,000 people had made entry, and the trains continued to pull in and out, loaded to the doors. Unlike the Lower Brulé Opening, there was no dreary standing in line for hours, even days, at a time. The seekers passed down the line like rapidly inspected herds.

And among them, inevitably, came the parasites who live on crowds—gamblers, crooks, sharks, pickpockets, and the notorious women who followed border boom towns. The pioneer towns were outraged, and every citizen automatically became a peace officer, shipping the crooks out as fast as they were discovered. They wouldn't, they declared virtuously, tolerate anything but "honest" gambling. And their own gambling rooms continued to run twenty-four hours a day.

In spite of precautions, not a few of the trusting folk from farms and small towns to whom this event was a carnival affair found themselves shorn like sheep at shearing time before they knew what was happening. One farm boy lost not only all his money but his fine team and wagon as well. A carnival it was, of course, in some respects. Amusement stands, in tents or shacks, lined the streets and never closed. Warnings came by letter to Superintendent Witten, describing crooks who were on their way to the Rosebud.

Motion pictures ran day and night, their ballyhoo added to the outcries of the other barkers. And the registration never stopped. Clerks and others employed as assistants by the government were hired in four-hour shifts. Post offices stayed open all night.

The government's headquarters were at Dallas, with a retinue of officials in charge. Thus the little town at the end of the North Western Railroad was the Mecca of that lottery. There the hysterical mob spirit appeared. And one day in the midst of the Opening, a prairie fire broke out, sweeping at forty miles an hour over the land the people had come to claim, sweeping straight toward Dallas. The whole town turned out to fight it—it had to. The Indians pitched in to help. And the tenderfeet, including reporters and photographers from the big city newspapers, turned fire fighters, fighting to save the town.

105

In spite of their efforts the fire reached the very borders of the town, destroying a few buildings. And at the sight of the flames the government employees caught up the great cans which contained the seekers' applications for the land and rushed them out of town toward safety. That day the cans contained 80,000 applications.

That great, black, charred area extending for miles over the prairie put a damper on the spirits of the locating agents. But these people had come for land, and they were not to be daunted. All over the great reservation groups could be seen investigating the soil, digging under the fire-swept surface, driving on into the regions of tall grass and scattered fields bordering the Rosebud. They were hoping to win a piece of that good earth.

As the close of the registration drew near, the excitement was intensified. Letters to Superintendent Witten poured in, asking him to hold back claims for people who were unable to register. The registration closed on October 17, 1908. No registrations would be accepted after a certain hour. Captain Yates, assistant superintendent of the Opening, started from O'Neill, Nebraska, bearing the applications from that registration point. So that there would be no danger of his not reaching the town of Dallas with the applications before the deadline, a special train was waiting for him. In his excitement Captain Yates rushed past the men waiting for him, crossed the track where his special was getting up steam, and took a train going the wrong way! Telegrams, another special train, cleared tracks—and he was finally able to rush in with his applications at the last moment.

Others were not so fortunate. Tired horses, a missed train connection, some unforeseen delay, and they arrived an hour, half an hour, perhaps only a few minutes after the registration had closed. Too late!

Oddly enough, one of the last to register was the foreman of the U Cross Ranch, who came galloping across the prairie at the last moment to make his application for a homestead. And when a ranchman turned to homesteading, that was news!

On October 19 the Drawing began. The government saw that every precaution must be taken to make sure of fair play; any suspicion of illegality might cause an uprising of the mob of a hundred thousand excited, disappointed people.

The great cans were pried open, and the applications put onto large platforms, where they were shuffled and mixed—symbolically enough with rakes and hoes—for it was quarter-sections of land they were handling.

From out the crowd applicants were invited onto the platform, and if one succeeded in selecting his own name he would be entitled to the first choice of land and location. Business firms, townsite companies were making open offers of $10,000 for Claim No. 1. Then two little girls, blindfolded, drew the sealed envelopes from the deep pile. Superintendent Witten opened them and announced the names to the crowd filling the huge tent where the Drawing was held.

The hushed suspense of that Drawing was like that of a regiment waiting to go over the top. The noisy excitement of registration was over. The people waited, tense and breathless, for the numbers to be called. Ironically enough, a great number of the winners had gone home. They would be notified by mail, of course. It was largely the losers who had waited.

The first winner to be present as his number was called was greeted with generous applause and cheers and demands for a speech. He was a farmer from Oklahoma, and instead of speaking, he felt in his pockets and held up, with a rather sheepish smile, a rabbit's foot which he had brought with him. Press agents stood by, waiting for the outcome. Daily newspapers printed the official list of the winners as the numbers came out, and all over the United States people waited for the announcement of the Rosebud's Lucky Numbers. The Rosebud had been opened up and swallowed by the advancing wave of people westward. But there was more land!

Fred Farraday drove me home from Presho, weary to the bone, and content to ride without speaking, listening to the steady clop-clop of the horses over that quiet road on which we did not meet a human being. And in my pocketbook $400, the proceeds from the sale of the postcards. Something, as Ida Mary had predicted, had happened.

Ma Wagor came in from the store. "Land sakes," she exclaimed, "you musta been through some confusement! You look like a ghost."

It didn't matter. "I have four hundred dollars. There will be another hundred or so when the agents finish checking up on the card sales, and I'll get a check from the News Service. It will pay the bills, and some left over to help us through the winter. We've saved the claim."

After a pause I added, "The Lower Brulé seems pretty small after the Rosebud. I'd like to go over there to start a newspaper."

"No," said Ida Mary. "You can't do that. Your claim and your newspaper and your job are here. After all, anyone can file on a claim. It's the people who stay who build the country."

X. THE HARVEST

I was pony-expressing the mail home one day when I saw a great eagle, with wings spread, flying low and circling around as though ready to swoop upon its prey. It was noon on a late fall day with no sight or sound of life except that mammoth eagle craftily soaring. I turned off the trail to follow its flight. It was the kind of day when one must ride off the beaten trail, when the sun is warm, the air cool and sparkling; even Lakota seemed like a stodgy animal riveted to the earth, and the only proper motion was that of an eagle soaring.

Abruptly the eagle swooped down into the coulee out of sight and came up a hundred yards or so in front of me, carrying with it a large bulky object. At the same instant a shot rang out, the eagle fell, and its bulky prey came down with a thud.

So intent was I upon the eagle that I was not prepared for what happened. At the shot Lakota gave a leap to the right and I went off to the left. I had no more than landed when a rider, whom I had seen lope up out of the coulee as the eagle fell, had my horse by the bit and was bending over me.

"Hurt?" he asked.

"I don't think so. Just scared," I replied as I got stiffly to my feet. The soft, thick grass had provided a cushioned landing place and saved my bones.

The stranger took a canteen from his saddle and gave me a drink of water; led the horses up to form a shade against the bright noon sun, and bade me sit quiet while he went back to see what the eagle had swooped down upon.

"A young coyote, just a pup," he announced upon his return. "I'm glad I got that fellah. They are an awful pest." It was a big bird with an eight-foot stretch from wing tip to tip as measured by this plainsman's rule—his hands. "They carry away lambs and attack new-born calves," he said. "They attack people sometimes, but that is rare."

He helped me on my horse. "All my fault. Couldn't see you from down in the coulee when I fired at that bird. You musta just tipped the ridge from the other side." He reached over, untied the mail bag and tied it to his saddle.

"You were going the other way, weren't you?" I protested.

"No hurry. I'll go back with you first."

"You don't know where I live, do you?"

"Yes, I know," he said laconically. He was a young man—I took him to be under thirty—with a sort of agile strength in every movement. Lean, virile, his skin sunburnt and firm. He wore a flannel shirt open at the throat, buckskin chaps, a plainsman's boots, and his sombrero was worn at an angle. He made no attempt to be picturesque as did many of the range riders.

As the horses started off at an easy gallop he checked them. "Better go slow after that shake-up," he said quietly.

"I must hurry," I answered. "I'm late with the mail."

"These homesteaders are always in a rush. Shore amusin'. Act like the flood would be here tomorrow and no ark built." He spoke in a soft, southern drawl.

"They have to do more than build an ark," I told him. "They have to make time count. The country is too new to accomplish anything easily."

109

"Too old, you mean. These plains have been hyar too long for a little herd of humans to make 'em over in a day."

"We have fourteen months to do it in," I reminded him, referring to the revised proving-up period.

"You'll be mighty sore and stiff for a few days," he said as he laid the mail sack down on the floor; "sorry, miss, I scared your horse," and touching his ten-gallon hat he was gone.

"Where did *he* hail from?" Ma Wagor demanded from the store where she had been watching.

"He's not from Blue Springs, Ma."

"I declare you are as tormentin' as an Indian when it comes to finding out things," Ma exclaimed in disappointment. She couldn't understand how I could have ridden any distance with the man without learning all about his present, guessing at his past, and disposing of his future to suit myself. People, as Ma frequently pointed out, were made to be talked to.

Just before sunset one day a week or so later I was sitting in the shop when the cowboy walked in. "Got to thinkin' you might be hurt worse than you appeared to be." He said he was top hand, had charge of a roundup outfit over in the White River country some fifty miles away, and some of the stock had roamed over on the reservation. Name was Lone Star—Lone Star Len.

And then one gray, chilly day in November, with the first feathery snowflakes, he rode up on his cow pony to say good-by. He was leaving the country, taking a bunch of cattle down to Texas for winter range. He was glad to be going. "Don't see how folks can live huddled up with somebody on every quarter-section. Homesteaders is ruinin' the country, makin' it a tore-up place to live. It's too doggone lonesome with all this millin' around."

When the Brulé became populated, Lone Star Len had gone into the empty Rosebud country, "where I'm not hemmed in by people, some place where there's a little room." Now he would be driven on— and on. And in the spring there would be a new influx of people in our section of the frontier.

Meanwhile, fall had come. The plains, which had stretched to the horizon that spring untouched by a plow, unoccupied by white men, were now unrecognizable. A hundred thousand acres of fertile waste land had been haltered. Hundreds of settlers had transplanted their roots into this soil and had made it a thriving dominion. Fall rains filled the dams and creeks. There were potatoes and other vegetables in abundance.

Think of it! Caves full of melons, small but sweet. *The Wand* told of one small field that yielded twenty bushels of wheat, another twenty-two bushels of oats, to the acre. There was fall plowing of more ground, schools being established, Sunday schools, preparations for the winter already in progress.

Never had a raw primitive land seen such progress in so short a time. And *The Wand* had played a substantial part in this development. It was swamped with letters of inquiry.

Fall was roundup time on the range. The Indian lands were so far-reaching that there were no nearby ranches, but the herds ranged over miles of territory around us.

And across the fence, on the unceded strip, the great herds of Scotty Phillips's outfit roamed over his own and the Indians' holdings. Across the plains came the ceaseless bawling of thousands of cows and calves being separated. That wild, mad, pitiful bawling rent the air and could be heard through the stillness of night for miles around, and the yelling and whooping of cowboys, the stamping of cow ponies and herds, the chanting and tom-toms of the Indians.

And enveloping it all, the infinite plains, unmoved, undisturbed by all that was taking place upon them.

So the homesteaders gathered their first harvest, and the goose hung high. There was hay—great stacks and ricks of it. Piles of yellow corn stacked like hay in barbed-wire enclosures or in granaries. To commemorate that first golden harvest, the pilgrims of the Lower Brulé celebrated their first Thanksgiving.

Seeing the stacks of grain that stood ready for threshing or for feeding in the straw, old man Husmann pointed to the field. "Mein Gott in Himmel! Vat I tell you? Das oats made t'irty bushels an acre. And flax. Mein Gott! She grow on raw land like hair on a hog's back. Back in Ioway we know notings about flax for sod crop." Dakota taught the United States that flax was the ideal sod crop.

The average yield of oats with late and slipshod sowing had been around fifteen bushels to the acre. Some fields of spring wheat had run fifteen bushels. And potatoes had fairly cracked the ground open. One settler, an experienced potato grower, had four acres that yielded 300 bushels. *The Wand* played that up in headlines for easterners to see.

Late-ripened melons lay on the ground, green and yellow—watermelons, muskmelons, golden pumpkins ready for the Thanksgiving pie. Over the Strip women and children were gathering them in against a sudden freeze. The reservation fairly subsisted on melons

111

that fall. Before the harvest the rations had been getting slim, with the settlers' money and food supply running low.

Women dried corn, made pumpkin butter and watermelon pickles, and put up chokecherries. A number of them had grown in their gardens a fruit they called ground cherries. This winter there would be baked squash and pumpkin pie.

So there was food for man and beast. And Scotty Phillips who owned what was said to be the largest buffalo herd in America killed a buffalo and divided it among the settlers, as far as it would go, to add to the Thanksgiving cheer of the Brulé. There was a genuine sense of fruition about that first harvest. Looking back to the empty plains as they had stretched that spring, the accomplishments of the homesteaders in one brief summer were overwhelming. There had been nothing but the land. Now a community had grown up, with houses and schools, and the ground had yielded abundantly.

In other ways our efforts had also borne fruit. There was to be a new bridge at Cedar Creek. From the fight *The Wand* had carried on, one would think that we were boring a Moffat tunnel through the Great Divide. And *The Wand* fought a successful battle with John Bartine over county division. It had come about when Senator Phillips came by one day during the summer on his way from Pierre to his ranch. "Scotty" Phillips, senator, cattleman and business man, was one of the Dakotas' most influential citizens. A heavyset man he was, with an unconscious dignity and a strong, kindly face; a squaw man—his wife was a full-blooded Indian who had retained many of her tribal habits. One day one would see the Senator ride past in his big automobile, and the next day his wife would go by, riding on the floor of the wagon on the way to the reservation to visit her relatives.

"I stopped in to see if you wanted to go to the county division meeting tomorrow at Presho," Senator Phillips said. "It's a rather important matter to the settlers. *The Wand* will represent those of the Lower Brulé, of course."

What was county division? We set out the next morning to find out. The county, it appeared, was becoming so thickly settled that the people of the western part wanted it divided, with a county seat of their own. We learned that Lyman County covered approximately 2500 square miles and the settlers of the extreme western part were 110 miles from the county seat, with no means of transportation. It sounded reasonable enough, and *The Wand* backed those who wanted county division.

The speaker for that little meeting was a slight and unassuming young man who was greeted with cheers.

"Who is he?" I asked Senator Phillips.

"Why that," he said, "is John Bartine!"

John Bartine was one of the most noted and romantic figures of the western plains. He had come west with a few law books packed in his trunk and no money, a young tenderfoot lawyer. He almost starved waiting for a case. There were no law cases, no real legal difficulties but cattle rustling, and nothing, apparently, that an inexperienced young easterner could do about that. But he persuaded stockmen who were being wiped out by the depredations of the rustlers to let him take their cases against these outlaw gangs. He had himself elected judge so that he could convict the thieves. And he had convicted them right and left until a band of rustlers burned down the courthouse in retaliation. But he kept on fighting, at the risk of his own life, until at last that part of the country became safe for the cattlemen.

After we had heard him talk we discovered that the county division problem was not as simple as it appeared at first. It wasn't merely a problem of dividing territory; division would increase the taxes, the non-divisionists said.

We hadn't thought of that. One did not pay taxes on the land, of course, until he got his deed, but there were other taxes to be paid, and the homesteaders felt they were developing resources for the nation at their own expense.

I did not know how to carry on a campaign like that, but *The Wand* put facts and figures before the settlers, to bring the situation clearly before them and let them do the deciding. When a frontier newspaper ran out of something to do, it could always enter a county division fight, as there were always counties to be divided as soon as they were settled up, many of them larger than our smaller New England States. And, so far as my own district was concerned, I had won this first battle with Judge Bartine. But the fight against the measure was so strong that Lyman County was not divided for several years.

Although the settlers had not been on the Brulé long enough to vote, office seekers kept coming through, asking the indorsement of *The Wand*. "It's no wonder the men we elect to run things make such a fizzle when they get into office," Ma Wagor snorted one day with impatience; "they wear themselves plumb out getting there."

Old Porcupine Bear, wise man and prophet, warned us that it would be a hard winter, and the plainsmen agreed that it was a humdinger. I asked the wise old Indian how he could foretell the winter.

"By food on shrub and tree," he said, "heap plenty; the heavy coat of the animals; the bear and squirrel storing heap much for eat, and the bear he get ready go sleep early." And so the winter came on us.

The dams froze over and the Strip was a great white expanse which appeared level at first sight but was beautifully undulating. Now there was a shack on every quarter-section, which appeared black in relief against the white. The atmosphere did curious things to them. Sometimes they looked like small dry-goods boxes in the distance, sometimes they seemed to have moved up to the very door. A coyote off a mile or two, or a bunch of antelope running along a ridge in the distance, appeared to be just across the trail.

In the mornings we cut a hole in the ice of our dam to dip out the water for household use, and then led the livestock down to drink. And at night we went skating on the larger dams, with the stars so large and near it seemed one could reach up and touch them, and no sound on the sleeping prairie but the howling of a pack of wolves down in the next draw.

But there were tracks on the white floor of earth, tracks of the living things which inhabit the silent areas and which had stealthily traveled across the plains, sometimes tracks of the larger wild beasts, and everywhere jack rabbits squatted deep in the snow.

The majority of the settlers wintered in little paper-shell hovels, of single thin board walls, the boards often sprung apart and cracked by the dry winds; a thin layer of tar paper outside and a layer of building paper on the inside, which as a rule was stretched across the studding to provide insulation between the wall and lining. Some of these paper linings were thin and light, the average settler having to buy the cheapest grade he could find.

We got along fairly well unless the wind blew the tar paper off. There was not a tree, not a weather-break of any kind for protection. Sometimes the wind, coming in a clean sweep, would riddle the tar paper and take it in great sheets across the prairie so fast no one could catch up with it. The covering on our shack had seen its best days and went ripping off at the least provocation. With plenty of fuel one could get along fairly well unless the tar paper was torn off in strips, leaving the cracks and knotholes open. Then we had to stop up the holes with anything we had, and patch the paper as best we could.

We had our piano out there that winter and Ida Mary bought a heating stove for the front room. "The Ammons girls are riding high," some of the settlers said good-naturedly. But when the stove, the cheapest listed in the mail-order catalog, arrived, Ida Mary cried with disappointment and then began to laugh. It was so small we could not tell whether it was a round heater or a bulge in the stovepipe. With it the temperature of the room ran automatically from roasting to freezing point unless one kept stoking in fuel.

In some ways Ida Mary and I remained objects of curiosity. Occasionally we saw indications of it. There had been a hot Sunday afternoon during the summer when Ida Mary and I were sitting in the open door of the shack. A strange cowboy rode up to the door. "Is this the place where the newspaper and everything is?"

We told him that it was. He threw one leg over the saddlehorn and fanned himself with his sombrero, looking us over, gaudy in a red and black checkered shirt, fringed leather chaps and bright green neckerchief.

"Well, you ain't the ones I heard about that's runnin' it, are you?" He seemed puzzled.

Yes, we were the ones. Anything he wanted?

"No. I'm a new wrangler over on Bad Horse creek—I come from Montana. Montana Joe, they call me. And a bunch of the punchers was just a wondering what you looked like; wanted me to come over and find out," he admitted candidly.

"But," and he stared disapprovingly at our slippered feet, "them don't look like range hoofs to me. They look like Ramblin' Rosie's." Ramblin' Rosie, it appeared, was a notorious dance-hall girl.

And about that time a Chicago newspaper came out, carrying a big headline story, complete with drawings, about our adventures in taming the frontier. It pictured Ida Mary and me with chaps and six-shooters; running claim-jumpers off our land and fighting Indians practically single-handed, plowing the land in overalls, two large, buxom, hardy girls. In fact, it had us shooting and tearing up the West in general. A friend sent us a copy and we laughed over it hysterically, marveling at this transformation of two girls who were both as timid as field mice, into amazons. We hid it quickly so that no one could see it, and forgot about it until long afterwards.

But we weren't the only girls on the plains with problems. A surprising number of homesteaders were girls who had come alone. They had a purpose in being there. With the proceeds of a homestead they could finish their education or go into business.

Many of these girls came from sheltered homes and settled out in the wilderness of plains, living alone in little isolated shanties out of reach of human aid in case of illness or other emergency. They had no telephones or other means of communication. Some of them had no means of transportation, walking miles to a neighbor in order to send to town for a little food or fuel, sometimes carrying buckets of water a mile or two over the plains. In winter they were marooned for days and nights at a stretch without a human being to whom they could speak, and nothing but the bloodcurdling cry of coyotes at night to keep them company.

They tried to prepare themselves for any situation so that they would neither starve nor freeze; with books and papers to read and the daily grinding routine of work to be done on every homestead, where each job required the effort and time of ten in modern surroundings, they managed to be contented. But it took courage.

In spite of the rigors of the winter, the settlers made merry. Our piano was hauled all over the Strip for entertainments. Barring storms or other obstacles, it was brought home the next day, perhaps not quite as good as when it went, but a piano scuffed or off-tune did not matter compared to the pleasure Ida Mary had that winter, going to parties and dancing. I did not always go along; my strength didn't seem to stretch far enough.

Sometimes a group of homesteaders would drive up to the settlement about sundown in a big bobsled behind four horses, the sled filled with hay, heavy blankets and hot bricks. We would shut up shop and the whole staff would crowd into the sled, Imbert tucking Ida Mary in warm and snug.

On cold winter evenings, when a gray-white pall encircled the earth like a mantle of desolation, three or four of the girls were likely to ride up, each with a bag of cooked food, to spend the night. One never waited to be invited to a friend's house, but it was a custom of the homestead country to take along one's own grub or run the risk of going hungry. It might be the time when the flour barrel was empty. So our guests would bring a jar of baked beans, a pan of fresh rolls, potato salad or a dried-apple pie; and possibly a jack rabbit ready baked. Jack rabbit was the main kind of fresh meat, with grouse in season. We had not as yet been reduced to eating prairie dog as the Indians did.

"Breaking winter quarantine," the girls would announce as they rode up.

Late in the evening we brought in the ladder, opened up the small square hole in the ceiling, and our guests ascended to the attic. On the floor next to the hole was a mattress made of clean, sweet, prairie hay. Our guest climbed the ladder, sat on the edge of the mattress, feet dangling down through the cubbyhole until she undressed, and then tumbled over onto the bed. The attic was entirely too low to attempt a standing posture.

On one such night with three girls stowed away in the attic, we lay in bed singing.

"Hello, hello there," came an urgent call.

We peered through the frosted window, trying to see through the driving snow, and made out a man on horseback.

"I'm on my way to Ft. Pierre and I am lost! I am trying to reach the Cedar Creek settlement for the night."

"You can't make it, stranger, if you don't know the country," Ida Mary called out.

"Well, what have I struck?" he asked, perplexed.

"A trading post."

"A trading post! It sounded like an opera house."

"We don't know who you are," Ida Mary called through the thin wall of the shack, "but you can't get on tonight in this snow. Tie your horse in the hayshed and we will fix you a bed in the store."

Next morning the girls rolled down the ladder one at a time, clothes in hand, to dress by the toy stove while Ida Mary and I started the wheels of industry rolling. When breakfast was ready we called in our strange guest.

When he asked for his bill we told him we were not running public lodgings but that we took in strangers when it was dangerous for them to go on.

After that Ida Mary always left a lamp burning low in the kitchen window, and the little print shop, set on the high tableland, served as a beacon for travelers who were lost on the plains.

Many a night stranded strangers sought shelter at the Ammons settlement. No other trading center in the middle of a reservation was run by girls, so strangers took it for granted that there were men about, or if they knew we were alone they did not think of our being unarmed in that country where guns had been the law.

Once we decided we should have a watchdog around. Ida Mary traded a bright scarf and some cigarettes for two Indian mongrels. They were lean and lopeared and starved. The only way they ever would halt an intruder was by his falling down over them, not knowing they were there. And they swallowed food like alligators. Van Leshout named them "Eat" and "Sleep." In indignation Ida Mary returned them to their owners. What was the matter, they wanted to know. "No barkum, no bitem," Ida Mary explained, and she tied them firmly to the back of the first Indian wagon headed for the Indian settlement and gave up the idea of a dog for protection.

However, women were probably safer in the homestead section than in any other part of the country. Women had been scarce there, and they met with invariable respect wherever they went; it was practically unheard of for a solitary woman to be molested in any fashion.

Both men and women came through the Strip that winter looking for friends or relatives who had claims, or in quest of land. Often they could get no farther than the print shop by nightfall. And never was any such person refused food or shelter.

Ida Mary went around that winter with one of the city boys, though she still saw Imbert. "We take each other too much for granted," she said. "I've been dependent upon him for companionship and diversion and help in many ways. For his sake and mine I must know that it's more than that."

I cannot recall that we ever planned ahead of proving up on the claim. We measured life by proving-up time. Only the dirt farmers planned ahead. And Ma Wagor—who was an inveterate matchmaker. I can see her now, driving across the plains, holding her head as high as that of the spotted pony she drove—a pony which, though blind as a bat, held its head in the air like a giraffe.

Often she would stay with us at night. "Pa won't mind. He's got plenty of biscuit left," she would say; "the cow give two gallons of milk today, and he's got *The Wand* and the Blue Springs paper to read—"

But sometimes, when business had kept her from home for two or three days, or we needed her, she would gaze out of the window, watching for him.

And it got colder. Getting the mail back and forth to the stage line became a major problem. "It appears to me," said Ma, "like a post office is as pestiferous a job as a newspaper." But Ma never admitted anything pestiferous about running the store.

The post office receipts picked up. Mail bags were jammed with letters written by the settlers through long, lonely evenings. The profits helped to pull us through as the newspaper business slumped to almost nothing during the "holing-in" period. The financial operations of the trading post, in fact, rose and fell like a Wall Street market.

We struggled through sharp wintry squalls to the stage line with the laden sacks of mail, and realized that when the winter really set in we would never be able to make it. So Dave Dykstra was appointed mail-carrier. He was a homesteader who taught the McClure school that winter, a slim, round-shouldered chap, rather frail in physique. Dave would never set the world on fire, but he would keep it going around regularly. Blizzard, rain or sun, he came to the post office every morning those short winter days before it was light. At night Ida Mary, as postmistress, would lock the mail sack and carry it into the cabin. In the morning we would hear Dave's sharp-shod horse striking the hard-frozen ground, and one of us would leap to the icy floor, wrap up in a heavy blanket, stick our feet into sheep-lined moccasins (some nights we slept in them), open the door a foot or so, and hold out the mail bag. Dave would grab it on the run.

One who has never tried it has no idea what that feat meant in a shell of a hut with the temperature ten or twenty degrees below zero, freezing one's breath in the performance. We used to hope Dave would oversleep, or that his coffee would fail to boil so that we might have a few more moments to sleep.

The Indians were always underfoot. The great cold did not keep them away. Men sauntered around, trading, loafing. Women sat on the floor, papooses on their backs, beadwork in hand. Our trade was extended to Indian shawls, blankets, moccasins and furs, for which the post found ready and profitable markets. Ida Mary became an adept at Indian trading. By that time we had a smattering of the Sioux language, although we were never really expert at it. It did not require much to trade with the Indians.

Often they turned their horses loose, built campfires and spent the day. They rolled a prairie dog in the wet earth, roasted it in the fire, and invited us to eat. They brought us *shanka*, dog meat. There was a time when we actually swallowed it because we were afraid to refuse. But now we shook our heads.

It was wood-hauling season, and women came sitting flat on the back end of loads. Among the Indian women were a few with primitive intelligence and wisdom. Others were morose and taciturn.

Even during the enforced lull of the deep winter there seemed to be much to do, and the routine duties of the post office and *The Wand* appeared to require most of our time. The opportunity to study, to know the Sioux, was at hand, but we never took advantage of it; like most people, we were too busy with the little things to see the possibilities around us. Perhaps Alexander Van Leshout, who made a success of his Indian art, came to know these people better than any of us. But he was an artist—and therefore he refused to let the little things clutter up his life and take his attention from the one thing that was important to him—seeing clearly and honestly the world about him.

When the Indians got their government pay, they celebrated with a buying spree. They were lavish buyers as long as they had a cent, and they bought the goods that had the most alluring picture on can or box. Ida Mary would hold up something of staple quality, but they would shake their heads and turn to something gaudily wrapped.

Old Two-Hawk and a few others paid their yearly subscriptions to *The Wand* every time they got their government allotment. "Your subscription is already paid," I would explain, but they would shake their heads and mutter. This was their newspaper, too, the thing that had signs and their own names printed on a machine. They had the right to trade beadwork or another dollar for it any time they liked.

Our subscription list looked like a Sioux directory with such names as Julia Lame Walking Eagle, Maggie Shoots at Head, Afraid of His Horses, Paul Owns the Fire, and his son, Owns the Fire.

Our daily visitors were the rank and file of the tribe, although famous old warriors and medicine men came now and then. The high rulers of the Brulé, who were among the most reserved and intelligent of all American Indians, did not come in this manner. But any negotiations between the Brulé whites and the Brulé red men were made with their Chief and Council. A few of the Indian warriors and chiefs always would hate the whites, but the rank and file of the Brulés were enjoying the strange new life about them. While they saw no advantage in an active life for themselves, they found activity in others highly entertaining.

The weather with its dry cold was sometimes deceptive. For several days we had had urgent business to attend to in Presho, but the weather prohibited the trip. One morning we awoke to see the sun brilliant on the snow.

A lovely day for the long trip, and we hitched the team to a light buggy so that we might wrap up better. The farther we drove the colder we became. There was no warmth in that dazzling sun. We huddled down as near as possible to the hot bricks. We took turns driving, one of us wrapped up, head and ears beneath the heavy robes.

On that whole journey we did not meet a soul. We were frozen stiff and had to have our hands thawed out in cold water when we reached Presho.

A homesteader living ten miles out stepped into the land office while we were there.

"Don't you girls know enough to stay at home on a day like this? I didn't dare attempt it until I saw you go by. I said to the family, 'There go the Ammons girls,' so I hitched up and started. And here it is 28 below zero."

The land commissioner said, "Well, you can't depend on the Ammons girls as a thermometer."

And the storms came.

XI. THE BIG BLIZZARD

Several miles from Ammons a bachelor gave a venison dinner on his claim to which a little group of us had gone. About noon it clouded up and no barometer was needed to tell us that a big storm was on the way. As soon as we had eaten we started home.

The sky was ominous. Antelope went fleeting by; a little herd of horses, heads high, went snorting over the prairie. Coyotes and rabbits were running to shelter and a drove of cattle belonging to the Phillips ranch were on a stampede. One could hear them bawling madly.

The guests had gone to the dinner together in a big wagon and were delivered to their respective shacks on the way back. We raced the horses ahead of the storm for a mile or two, but it was upon us by the time we reached Margaret Houlihan's. As we drove on up the draw to the settlement we saw the chimney of our cabin, consisting of a joint of stovepipe (the regulation chimney in this country) go flying across the prairie. And there was not an extra joint of pipe on the place—probably not one on the reservation, which meant that we would not be able to build a fire in the house until we could go to Presho or the state capital for a joint.

"Hey, whata you goin' to do," exclaimed the young neighbor boy who had taken us to the dinner. "You can't live in your shack through the storm that's comin' without a fire."

"We have a monkey-stove in the store," Ida Mary told him. He shook his head, but before hurrying home he scooped up a few buckets of coal we had on hand and took it into the store, and watered and fed the horses, knowing we might not be able to reach them until the blizzard had passed. "That all the fuel you got?" he demanded.

"A settler went to town this morning to get coal for us."

"But he can't get back until the storm is over. How you goin' to manage? No fire in your shack? No fuel for the monkey-stove?"

"We'll be all right," we assured him. He was not convinced, but he dared not linger. He had to get home while he could still find the way.

In thirty minutes we were completely shut in by the lashing force of wind and snow that swept across the plains in a blinding rage. Ma Wagor and Kathryn, our typesetter, had gone home and we were alone, Ida Mary and I. We built up a hot fire in the monkey-stove, which sat in the middle of the store building and was used for heating both store and print shop. From canned goods on the shelf, baked beans and corned beef, we prepared a sketchy supper, and ate on the counter.

Although it had been without heat only a few hours, the shack was already like an iceberg, and we were shaking with cold by the time we managed to drag the couch out of it, with a mighty effort, and into the store. It was warm there, and we lay safe under warm blankets listening tranquilly to the storm hurling its strength furiously against the frail defense of the little store, the shriek of the wind, the beating of the snow on the roof. It must be horrible to be out in it, we thought, pleasantly aware of protection and warmth and safety.

Next morning there was a real old-time blizzard raging. We could barely see the outline of the shack ten feet from the store; the rest of the world was blotted out and the wind roared like an incoming tide as the snow and sleet pelted like shot on the low roof. A primeval force drove the storm before it. All over the plains people were hemmed in tar-paper shacks, the world diminished for them to the dimensions of their thin-walled houses, as alone as though each were the only dweller on the prairie.

The team, Fan and Bill, and Lakota were the only horses tied up in the hay barn. They could reach the hay and eat snow for water. There would be plenty of snow. Our menagerie of Indian plugs, including Pinto, was loose on the plains; but they were accustomed to battling storms in the open and there were haystacks now to provide food and shelter. Somewhere in the open they were standing, huddled together, facing the onslaught of the storm.

The west end wall of the flimsy ell print shop, exposed to the full force of the storm, was swaying in. Together we dragged forth some boxes of canned goods, heavy cans of lard and molasses, and propped it with their weight. We watched anxiously for a time, but the heavy boxes seemed to provide sufficient support. There were no further signs of the wall collapsing.

By evening the storm had gripped the plains like a demon of wrath. We had been rather enjoying this seclusion—no Indians. And— we chuckled like a victim of persecution whose persecutor had been overtaken—there would be no mail carrier in the morning. No mail to be taken care of. Exultant, we tried to figure how many days Dave would be blockaded and we would be spared that morning penance of handing the mail sack out from the icy shack.

On the second morning the storm was still raging, with the snow two feet deep between the store and the barn. The west wall still held, and between glances at it we stoked the monkey-stove. Stoked it while the coal dwindled. When the last chunk had been swallowed up we hunted around for something else to burn. Newspapers, cartons, wooden boxes—everything we could find went into the voracious maw of the stove.

We tended it as religiously as priestesses at an altar, or as primitive men building up a fire to keep off wild animals. Only under such conditions does one fully experience that elemental worship of fire. It literally meant life to us.

Searching for something else we could burn, something else to keep that flame going even a little while longer, that pleasant glow which had come with our sense of protection gradually disappeared. The blizzard was not merely a gigantic spectacle put on by nature for our entertainment, it was a menace, to be kept at bay only by constant alertness on our part.

Now there was nothing left in the store that we could burn!

"The Indians brought some fence posts," Ida Mary recalled. "They are back of the barn where they unloaded them. We'll have to get them."

We put on our coats, pulled fur caps close down around our faces and ears, wrapped gunny sacks around our feet and legs over high arctics to serve as snowshoes. It took our combined strength to push the door open against the storm. Before we could close it behind us, snow had swept into the store and was making little mounds. Clinging to each other we plowed our way through the loose snow to the fence posts and dragged in a few, making two trips, breaking a trail with them as we went. The wind-blown snow cut our faces like points of steel. Hearing the restless whinny of the horses, we stopped to untie them. They would not go far from shelter.

Naturally the fence posts were much too long to go into the stove, and we had no way of chopping them up. So we lifted up a cap of the two-hole stove and stuck one end of a post into the fire, propped the other end up against the counter, and fed the fire by automatic control. When one post burned down to the end, we stuck in another. It seemed to us that they burned awfully fast, and that the store was getting colder and colder. We put on our heavy coats for warmth and finally our overshoes.

Storm or no storm, however, *The Wand* had to be printed. We pulled the type-case into the store, close to the stove. In those heavy coats and overshoes we went to work on the newspaper—and that issue was one of the best we ever published. In those two long nights, shut off from all the world, we talked and planned. We dared not take the risk of going to bed. If we should sleep and let the fire go out, we were apt to freeze, so we huddled around the stove, punching fence posts down into the fire, watching the blaze flicker.

At least there was time to look ahead, time to think, time to weigh what we had done and what we wanted to do. So that week *The Wand* came out with ideas for cooperative action that were an innovation in the development of new lands, a banded strength for the homesteader's protection. It seemed logical and simple and inevitable to me then—as it does now. "Banded together as friends"—the Indian meaning of Lakota—was the underlying theme of what I wanted to tell the homesteaders. The strength and the potentialities of one settler counted for little, but—banded together!

Our enthusiasm in planning and talking carried us through most of that day. But toward evening there were more immediate problems. It began to turn bitter cold. The very air was freezing up. It was no

125

longer snowing, but the wind had picked up the snow and whirled it over the prairie into high drifts that in places covered up the barbed-wire fences against which it piled.

And under the piling snow our fuel lay buried; a long windrow drift had piled high between the posts and the shop. And the shop was growing colder and colder. Even with the heavy coats and overshoes we stamped our feet to keep out the chill and huddled over the dying fire. It would soon be freezing cold in the store, as cold as the icy shack which we had abandoned. No wonder people worshiped fire!

There was no sense of snug protection against the storm now. It seemed to have invaded the store, although the west wall still held. "We'll have to go somewhere for warmth," Ida Mary decided. Margaret's shack was the nearest, but even so we knew the grave risk we took of perishing on the way there. Action, however, is nearly always easier than inaction. A time or two we stuck our heads out of the door and the cold fairly froze our breath. Once I went outside, and when I tried to get back into the shack the wind, sucking between the few buildings, blew me back as though an iron hand held me.

"If we stay here," we thought, "we may be walled in by morning by the fast-drifting snow." So we decided on Margaret's, a quarter-mile down the draw. The chief difficulty was that the trip must be made against the storm, and we did not know whether we could make it or not. We each wrapped up tightly in a heavy Indian shawl, tied ourselves together with a light blanket, picked up the scoop shovel, and started down the buried trail.

Out through the side door and the narrow space between the buildings which had been protected against the drifts, we made our way; then, facing the full strength of the storm, we dug our way, shoveling as we went, through a drift that had piled in front of the buildings, and on through the deep level of snow.

It was getting dark now—the sudden steel-gray that envelops the plains early on a winter night and closes in around the white stretches, holding them in a vise. The only sign of life in the whole blanketed world was the faint glimmer of light in Margaret's window. We knew now how the light in the print shop must have looked many a night to strangers lost on the prairie in a storm.

Such lightweights were we that, at every step we took, the wind blew us back; we used all our force, pushing against that heavy wall of wind, until we struck drifts that almost buried us. For all our clumsy tying, the blanket held us together or we would have lost each other. We could not speak, because if we so much as parted our lips they seemed to freeze to our teeth, and the cold wind rasped in our throats and lungs as though we had been running for a very long time.

Had the snow been tightly packed we could never have dug our way out of some of the drifts. But it had been picked up and swirled around so much by the wind that it was loose and light. It blew up off the ground, lashed against our faces like sharp knives, and blinded us. "How horrible," we had thought from the shelter of the store, "to be out in the storm." But we hadn't tasted then the malignant fury of the thing, battling with us for every step we made.

At last we turned and walked backwards, resting on the shovel handle for fear we would fall from exhaustion. Every few steps we looked around to see whether we were still going in a straight line toward the dim light that shone like a frosted glimmer from the tiny shack which now looked like a dark blur. We realized that if we were to swerve a few feet in either direction, so that we lost sight of the lamp, we would not find Margaret's shack that night.

It was quite dark now, and no sound on the prairie but the triumphant howl of the wind and the dry crunch of our overshoes on the snow, slipping, stumbling. We were pushing ourselves on, but our feet were so numb it was almost impossible to walk. We had been doing it for hours, it seemed; we had always been fighting our way through the deep snow. The store we had left seemed as unreal as though we had never known its protection.

Ida Mary, still walking backwards, stumbled and fell. She had struck Margaret's shack. I pushed against the door, too numb to turn the knob.

The door opened and Margaret, with a cry, pulled us in. Swiftly she unbundled us, taking care not to bring us near the fire. She took off our gloves and overshoes, then ran to the door and scooped up a basin of snow for our numb hands and feet, snow which felt curiously warm and comforting. While the snow drew out the frost, she hastened about, making strong, hot tea.

While we drank the tea and felt warmth slowly creeping over us, "Why on earth did you attempt to come here on a night like this?" she demanded. "You might have frozen to death."

"We were out of fuel," we told her. "We had to take the chance."

The shack was cheerful and warm. There was a hot supper and fuel enough to last through the storm. Only a refuge for which one has fought as Ida Mary and I fought to reach that tar-paper shack could seem as warm and safe as Margaret's shack seemed to us that night. In a numb, delicious lethargy we sat around the stove, too tired and contented to move.

Safe from the fury of the wind, we listened to it raging about the cabin as though cheated of its victims. And then, toward midnight, it died away. There was a hush as though the night were holding its breath, and then the sky cleared, the stars came out.

The next day Margaret's brother took up a sack of coal on his bronco, so we made our way back over the trail we had broken the night before, to the store, and he built a fire for us. Later that same morning Chris rode over with a sack of coal tied on behind the saddle.

"Yoost in case you should run out once," he said as he brought it in. "My wife she bane uneasy when she see no light last night."

When we told him what had happened he shook his head in concern and went to work. He scooped a path to the barn and attended to the horses. From under the snow he got some fence posts which he chopped up while Charlie excavated an opening to the front door—in case anyone should be mad enough to try to reach the store on a day like that.

About noon a cowboy came fighting his way through the drifts in search of lost cattle which the storm must have driven in this direction—the only soul who dared to cross the plains that day.

It was Sourdough. I never knew his real name. I doubt if those with or for whom he worked knew.

He stopped at the print shop to rest his horse, which was wringing wet with sweat, though the day was piercing cold. He threw the saddle blanket over the horse and came in.

We begged him to go and find out whether or not the Wagors were all right. After Ida Mary and I had got straightened out, it occurred to us that they had sent in their order for coal with ours. Like us they might be imprisoned in their shack and low on fuel; but, unlike us, there would be no question of their battling their way across the prairie to shelter.

"Sufferin' sinners," grumbled Sourdough. "Think I got time to fool around with homesteaders when a bunch of critters is maybe dead or starvin' to death? Godamighty!"

We argued and insisted, telling him that he knew better how to break a trail than the tenderfeet around here, that his horse was better trained for it.

"This country warn't made for no humans—just Indians and rattlesnakes and cowhands is all it was intended for."

I agreed with him. I was ready to agree with anything he might say if he would only go to the Wagors' shack. At last, after we had exhausted all the wiles and arts of persuasion at our command, Ida Mary told him that, come to think of it, she had seen a bunch of cattle drifting in the direction of the Wagor claim. He started out, saying he might stop in if he happened to drift by and it "come handy."

Sourdough found the Wagors covered up in bed. They had been in bed two days and three nights. The fuel had given out, as we had feared—cow chips and all. They had burned hay until the drifts became so high and the stack so deeply covered that the poor old man could no longer get to it. The cow and the blind horse had barely enough feed left to keep alive.

Not daring to burn the last bit of hay or newspaper—which would not have warmed the house anyhow—the old couple had gone to bed, piling over them everything that could conceivably shut out that penetrating dead cold, getting up just long enough to boil coffee, fry a little bacon and thaw out the bread. They dipped up snow at the door and melted it for water. The bread had run out, and the last scrap of fuel. They tore down the kitchen shelf, chopped it up, and the last piece of it had gone for a flame to make the morning coffee. The little snugly built shack was freezing cold. A glass jar of milk in the kitchen had frozen so hard that it broke the jar.

When Sourdough walked in and learned the situation he bellowed, "Sufferin' sinners!" and tore out like a mad steer. He cut into the haystack, cut up a few posts from the corral fence and made a fire—and when a range rider makes a fire it burns like a conflagration.

He fed the two dumb animals (meaning the cow and horse, he explained, though they weren't half as dumb as anyone who would go homesteading) while Ma stirred up some corn cakes and made coffee for them all. Milk the cow? What the hell did they think he was, a calf? Sourdough, like most cowboys, had never milked a cow. The only milk he ever used came out of a can.

Mid-afternoon he reported. When we wondered what could be done next, he said carelessly, "Godamighty! Let 'em stay in bed. If they freeze to death it will serve 'em right for comin' out here."

Grumbling, ranting on, he slammed the door and strode out to the barn, saddled Bill—the stronger horse of the brown team—and led him to the door.

"What are you going to do?" I demanded.

"Ride this no-count plug of yourn to hunt them critters. You never saw a bunch goin' that way," he accused Ida Mary. She smiled at the ruse she had used to start him out.

He jumped on Bill, leading his cow pony behind—a range rider knows how to conserve a horse's strength—and followed the trail he had broken, straight back toward the Wagor shack. Now we knew. He was going after Ma and Pa. They would be warm and nourished, with strength for the trip, and good old Bill could carry them both.

A few days later when we asked Ma about the harrowing experience she laughed and said, "Oh, it wasn't so bad. Pa and I talked over our whole life in those three days, telling each other about our young days; Pa telling me about some girls he used to spark that I never woulda heard about if it hadn't been for that blizzard.... I told him about my first husband ... he's the one who left me the ant-tic broach ... we did get pretty cold toward the last.

"I burned up every old mail-order catalog I had saved. I always told Pa they would come in handy.... What? Afraid we would freeze to death? Well, we woulda gone together."

The blizzard was over, but the snow lay deep all over the prairie and the great cold lasted so that few of the settlers ventured outside their shacks. For days there was no hauling done. The trails that had been worn since spring were buried deep and the drifts were treacherous. There were many homesteaders over the Reservation who were running out of fuel.

Now, if ever, was a time for cooperation, and *The Wand* printed a list of those who could spare fuel; they would share with those in need of it. They brought what they could to the settlement and pooled it, chopping up all the poles and posts they could find into stovewood, and taking home small loads to tide them over.

With the fury of that storm, one of the hardest blizzards the frontier had experienced, the winter spent itself. Under the soft warm breath of a chinook the snow disappeared like magic, melting into the soil, preparing it for the onslaught of the plow.

XII. A NEW AMERICA

Ida Mary and I came through the winter stronger than we had ever been before, but we welcomed the spring with grateful hearts. Only poets can describe the electric, sweet quality of spring, but only the young, as we were young that year, receive the full impact of its beauty. The deep, cloudless blue of western skies, the vivid colors after the dead white of winter, were fresh revelations, as though we had never known them before.

One spring day I was making up the paper, while the Christophersons' little tow-headed boy watched me.

"Are you going to be a printer when you grow up, Heine?"

"Nope. I don't want no little types," he replied. "I like traction machines better—they go. My Pa's got one."

A tractor coming on the Strip! I ran to tell Ida Mary.

As it chugged and caterpillared from town through the Reservation, Chris Christopherson's tractor caused almost as much excitement as the first steamship up the Hudson. Men, women and children gathered about and stared wide-eyed at the new machine as its row of plows cut through the stubborn sod like a mighty conqueror. He was plowing a hundred acres.

A few cattlemen from the open country rode into the Strip to see it and bowed their heads to this evidence of the coming of agriculture.

Old Ivar Eagleheart, Two-Hawk, and others of the Indian braves looked on. This mystic power sealed their fate. It was in a last desperate attempt to save territory for his race that an old Indian chief had stood indomitable, contending with the White Fathers. "Wherever you find a Sioux grave, that land is ours!" In this plowing up of the Indians' hunting grounds no one thought of Sioux graves.

The McClure homesteaders had filed on their claims, proved up and gone, many of them, leaving empty shacks. Here on the Strip were increasing signs of permanency. Many Brulé settlers went back home and disposed of whatever property they had in order to make permanent improvements on their claims. Other machinery came. Within a radius of three miles of Ammons three tractors ran all day. All night one could see their bright headlights moving and hear their engines chug-chugging over the dark plain, turning under the bluebells and anemones as they went, and the tall grass where buffalo had ranged. Fragrant scent of wild flowers blended with the pungent odor of new-turned earth and floated across the plain. When those owning tractors got through breaking for themselves they turned over sod for other settlers.

In every direction on the Brulé and all over the plains which had been settled, teams went up and down, making a black and green checkerboard of the prairie.

Ida Mary and I had Chris break and sow sixty acres of our land to flax. It cost $300, and we again stretched our credit to the breaking point to borrow the money. Try out fifteen or twenty acres first? Not we! If we had a good crop it would pay for the land.

The winners in the Rosebud Drawing were swarming onto their claims, moving their families and immigrant goods in a continuous stream. Towns for many miles around were deluged with trade. It was estimated that the Rosebud alone would add 25,000 new people to the West, with the settlers' families, tradesmen and others whom the Rosebud development would bring. A few groups of settlers from Chicago and other cities came with a fanfare of adventure new to the homestead country. But many stolid, well-equipped farmers, too, went into Tripp County, in which the Rosebud lay.

I got a letter from the Chicago reporter saying: "I did not draw a Lucky Number, but I came in on the second series to take the place of those who dropped out. Am out on my land and feeling better. It was sporting of you to offer to find a claim for me. Things are moving fast on the Rosebud."

Word spread that homesteaders were flocking farther west in Dakota—to the Black Hills—and on to the vast Northwest. That inexorable tide was pressing on, taking up the land, transforming the prairie, forcing it to yield its harvest, shaping the country to its needs, creating a new empire.

We peopled and stocked the West by rail—and put vast millions in the hands of the railroads. Wagon caravans moved on from the railroad into the interior, many going as far as fifty, sixty, a hundred miles over a trailless desert. Homesteaders who had no money and nothing to haul, came through in dilapidated vehicles and lived in tents until they got jobs and earned money to buy lumber. A few came in automobiles. There were more cars seen in the moving caravans now.

It was not only settlers the railroads carried west now, it was tools and machinery and the vast quantities of goods needed for comfort and permanent occupation; and the increasing demand for these materials was giving extra work to factories and businesses in the East.

On the Brulé we watched the growth of other sections of the West. At home alone one evening, Ida Mary had carried her supper tray outdoors, and as she sat there a rider came over the plains; she could barely recognize him in the dusk.

"Lone Star!" she exclaimed as he stopped beside her.

He sat silent, dejected, looking over the broad fields. He had brought the herd north to summer pasture.

"Did you escape the pesky homesteaders by going south?" she laughed.

"No," he said soberly. "They're all over. Not near as thick as they are here, but Colorado and New Mexico are getting all cluttered up. Old cattle trails broke—cain't drive a herd straight through no more—why—" he looked at her as though some great calamity had befallen, "I bet there's a million miles o' ba'b wire strung between here and Texas! Shore got the old Brulé tore up."

She laughed. "Better not let my sister hear you say that. Look at our crop coming up."

"I didn't think you'uns would stick it out this winter," he said.

"Most of the settlers stayed," she assured him.

"Looks like the end of the free range," he said. "Cattle business is going to be different from now on." He smiled wanly and asked for his mail, which consisted only of a pile of back-number copies of a newspaper. He took them and rode "off to the southeast," the vague description he had given us as to where he belonged.

But he had brought news. The stream of immigration was flowing in to the south and west of us, into country which was talked of as more arid and more barren than this tall grass country. The barb-wire told the story.

The United States had entered an era of western development when the homesteaders not only settled the land, but moved together, acted together, to subdue the land. It was an untried, hazardous venture on which they staked everything they had, but that is the way empires are built. And this vast frontier was conquered in the first two decades of the twentieth century; a victory whose significance has been almost totally ignored by historical studies of the country, which view the last frontier as having vanished a generation or more before.

Iron trails pushed through new regions; trails crossing the network of new civilization broadened into highways, and wagon tracks cut their way where no trails ever led before. New towns were being built. Industry and commerce were coming in on the tidal wave. A new America!

No cut-and-dried laws, no enforced projects or programs of a federal administration could possibly achieve the great solid expansion which this voluntary land movement by the masses brought about naturally.

It takes almost every commodity to develop a vast dominion that has lain empty since Genesis. It took steel for railroads, fences, and plowshares. It took lumber and labor—labor no end, in towns and out on the land. It took farm machinery, horses, harness, stoves, oil, food and clothing to build this new world.

I was delighted when one day there came a letter from Halbert Donovan, the New York broker. It contained great news for *The Wand*. And there was a little personal touch that was gratifying.

"We are beginning to feel the effect of a business expansion back here," he wrote, "which the western land development seems to be bringing about. If it continues, with all the public domain that is there, it is bound to create an enormous demand in industry and commerce. And I emphasize the statement I made to you that it is a gigantic project which a government alone could finance, and which requires the work of powerful industrial corporations.

"But, looking over that desolate prairie, one wonders how it can be done; or if it is just a splurge of proving up and deserting. However, it is surprising what these homesteaders are doing, and it is ironic that a little poetic dreamer should have foreseen the trend which things are taking. And I feel you deserve this acknowledgment. How in the name of God have you and your sister stuck it out?"

The reason that Halbert Donovan was interested in the progress of this area, I learned, was that his company had mining investments in the Black Hills and it was investigating a proposed railroad extension through the section.

The expansion which was beginning to be felt across the continent grew for five years or more up to the beginning of the World War, and then took another spurt after the war. It was not merely a boom, inflation to burst like a bubble. It grew only as more territory was settled and greater areas of land were put under cultivation.

"Do you know what we need out here most of all?" I said to Chris Christopherson one day, having in mind a settlers' bank.

"Yah, yah!" Chris broke in, his ruddy features beaming in anticipation. "A blacksmith shop! More as all else, we need that. Twenty-five miles we bane goin' to sharpen a plowshare or shod a horse yet."

Trade, business, industry? Yes, of course. But first the plow must pave the way. During those years money flowed from the farm lands rather than to them. The revenue from the homestead lands was bringing millions into the Treasury.

That spring the newspaper office became a clearing house for homestead lands. People wanting either to buy or sell relinquishments came there for information. All kinds of notices to be filed with the Department of the Interior were made out by the office, which began to keep legal forms in stock. Gradually I found myself becoming an interpreter of the Federal Land Laws and settlers came many miles for advice and information.

The laws governing homesteading were technical, with many provisions which gave rise to controversy. I discovered that many of the employees in the Department knew nothing of the project except the letter of the law. Through my work in handling proofs I was familiar with the technicalities. From actual experience I had learned the broader fundamental principles as they could be applied to general usage.

135

I became a sort of mediator between the homesteader and the United States Land Office. It was a unique job for a young woman and brought my work to the attention of officials in Washington and several Congressional public land committees. Slowly I was becoming identified with the land movement itself, and I had learned not to be overawed by the fact that some of the government's under-officials who came out to the Strip did not agree with my opinions. I had clashed already with several of them who had been sent out to check up on controversies in which the homesteaders' rights were disputed. They knew the technicalities better, perhaps, than I did; but in regard to conditions on the frontier they were rank amateurs and I knew it.

Land on the Brulé was held at a premium and landseekers were bidding high for relinquishments. So attractive were the offers that a few settlers who were hard pressed for money, sold their rights of title to the land, and passed it on to others who would re-homestead the claims. Several early proof-makers sold their deeded quarters, raw, unimproved, miles from a railroad, for $3000 to $3700 cash money.

Real estate dealers of Presho, Pierre, and other small towns looked to the Brulé as a plum, trying to list relinquishments there for their customers. But I got the bulk of the business! One of the handy men around the place sawed boards and made an extra table with rows of pigeonholes on it, and we installed this in the back end of the print shop for the heavy land-office business.

Most of our work on land affairs was done free in connection with the legal work of the newspaper. Then buyers or sellers of relinquishments began paying us a commission, and one day Ida Mary sold a claim for spot cash and got $200 for making the deal. Selling claims, she said, was as easy as selling *shela* (tobacco) to the Indians. The difficulty lay in finding claims for sale.

The $200 went to Sedgwick at the bank on an overdue note. He had moved into a bank building now, set on a solid foundation, instead of the rolling sheep wagon whose only operating expense was the pistols.

That entire section of the frontier was making ready for the incoming torrent of the Rosebud settlers to take possession of their claims. Droves of them landed at Presho early, reawakening the town and the plains with a new invasion. Thousands who had not won a claim followed in their wake, and everyone, when he had crossed the Missouri River, heard about the Brulé.

The government sent out notice for the appointment of a regular mail carrier for the Ammons post office. Dave Dykstra had resigned to farm his land, and Sam Frye, a young homesteader with a family, was appointed.

We began to need more printing equipment to carry on the increased newspaper business and to take care of the flood of proofs which would come in that summer; there was interest and a payment on the press coming due. So there was a day when Ida Mary said we were going to go under, unless we could do some high financing within thirty days.

"Oh, we'll get through somehow," I assured her. "It's like a poker game; you never know what kind of hand you will hold in the next deal." Planning ahead didn't help much, because something unexpected usually happened.

But no matter what hard luck a homesteader had or how much he had paid the government, unless he could meet the payments and all other requirements fully he lost the land and all he had put into it. We could not afford to lose our claim, so I concentrated on my Land Office business.

As usual, something happened. I was sitting in the private office of the United States Land Commissioner in Presho when a man walked into the front office and put a contest on a piece of land. I heard the numbers repeated through the thin partition and I knew exactly where the land lay; it was a quarter-section south of us on the reservation, which belonged to a young man who had to abandon it because he was ill and penniless. He had got a leave of absence which had run out, and he had no funds to carry on and prove up the claim. Yet he had put into the gamble several hundred dollars and spent almost a year's time on it. Now he was to lose it to the man who had contested it.

Nothing could be done to save the land for the man who had gone home; he had forfeited it. I started from my chair. The contest must be filed in Pierre. If I could get one in first, I could help out the man whose illness had deprived him of his land, and help out the ailing Ammons finances. But it would be a race!

Through the outer office I rushed while the land agent called after me, "Just a minute, Edith!"

"I'll be back," I told him breathlessly. "I'll be back. I just thought of something!"

I made the trip from Presho to Ammons in record time, raced into the post office and filled out a legal form with the numbers I had heard through the thin wall. But I needed someone not already holding a

137

claim to sign it, and there wasn't a soul at the settlement who would do.

It was getting dark when Ida Mary finally announced jubilantly that someone was coming from the direction of the rangeland. It was Coyote Cal, thus called because "he ran from the gals like a skeered coyote."

Talking excitedly, I dragged him into the print shop to sign the paper. "I don't want any doggone homestead pushed off onto me," he protested.

I thrust the paper into his hands. "It won't obligate you in any way," I explained.

"All right," he agreed. He enjoyed playing jokes and this one amused him. "But you're sure I won't get no homestead?"

Coyote poised the pen stiffly in his hand. "Let's see," he murmured in embarrassment, "it's been so gosh-darn long since I signed my name—danged if I can recollect—" the pen stuck in his awkward fingers as he swung it about like a lariat.

Finally he wrote laboriously "Calvin Aloysius Bancroft."

With the signed paper in my hands I saddled Lakota and streaked off for the thirty-five-mile trip to Pierre.

Late that night a tired horse and its rider pulled up in front of a little hotel in Ft. Pierre. I routed a station agent out of bed and sent a telegram to the young man who had left his claim.

Next morning when the U. S. Land Office at Pierre opened its door the clerks found me backed up against it with a paper in my outstretched hand. Half an hour later, when the morning mail was opened at the Land Office, there was a contest in it filed at Presho. But I had slapped a contest on the same quarter-section first, a contest filed by one Calvin Aloysius Bancroft, a legal applicant for the claim.

In the mail I received a signed relinquishment for the land from the young man, withdrew the contest and sold the relinquishment, which is the filer's claim to the land, for $450. I had made enough on the deal to meet our own emergencies and had saved $200 for the young man who needed it badly.

And *The Wand* was still safe. All around us the land was being harnessed, a desert being conquered with plowshares as swords.

Scotty Phillips stopped in at the print shop on his way from Pierre, where he lived, to his ranch. "The stockmen have been asleep," he said. "They ridiculed the idea that the range could ever be farmed. And now they are homesteading, trying to get hold of land as fast as they can. I have Indian lands leased, so I am all right."

As a squaw man he naturally owned quite a bit of land, a piece for each child, and he had three children.

Panicky, some of the stockmen filed on land, but a homestead for them was just big enough for the ranch buildings and corrals; it still did not allow for the essential thing—large range for the cattle. They began to buy from homesteaders and lease lands around them. For years the livestockman of the West had been monarch of all he surveyed, and the end of his reign was in sight. Like all classes of people who have failed to keep step with the march of progress, he would have to follow the herd.

A strong spirit of cooperation and harmony had developed among the army of the Brulé. They worked together like clockwork. There was little grumbling or ill-will. Just how much *The Wand* had done in creating this invaluable asset to a new country I do not know, but it was a factor. We were a people dependent upon one another. Ours was a land without established social law or custom. It was impossible to regulate one's life or habits by any set rule; and there was no time or energy for idle gossip or criticism. Each one had all he could do to manage his own business.

I had been working at high pressure, and as summer came on again I went back to St. Louis for a few weeks of rest, back down the Mississippi on the Old Bald Eagle to find my father waiting at the dock. I had half expected to find the family awaiting roaring stories of the West; instead, they listened eagerly and asked apt questions about soil and costs and the future. Things weren't going well for them. Perhaps for my father and the two small boys the future would point west.

I was surprised to find the general interest that people in St. Louis were taking in the West and in homesteading. Its importance, something even of its significance, was coming to be realized. They asked serious questions and demanded more and more information about the land. Business men talked about new opportunities there. "Bring lots of new business, this land movement," I heard on many sides.

After those long months of struggle for the bare necessities, I was greatly struck by lavish spending. It seemed startling to one from pioneer country. Where did the money come from, I wondered, that city folk were spending like water? I had come to think of wealth as coming from the land; here people talked of capital, stocks and bonds; occasionally of trade expansion. Surely this western development, I protested, was responsible in part for trade expansion. Ida Mary had said I ran to land as a Missourian did to mules; for the first time I began to consider it as an economic issue.

I was restless during my stay in St. Louis; the city seemed to have changed—or perhaps I had changed—and I was glad to get back home. It was the first time I had called the West home.

Unbelievably unlike my first sight of the desolate region, I found it a thriving land of farms and plowed fields, of growing crops and bustling communities, whose growth had already begun to affect the East, bringing increased business and prosperity, whose rapid development and far-reaching influence people were only slowly beginning to comprehend.

All this had been achieved in less than two years, without federal aid, with little money, achieved by hard labor, cooperation, and unquenchable hope

.

XIII. THE THIRSTY LAND

"You'd better do a little exhortin'," Ma told me on my return to the claim. "And if you get any collections, turn some of them in for the good of the store."

"Isn't business good?"

"Business is pouring in. It's money I'm talking about; there won't be any money until the crops are threshed—which will be about Christmas time out here. Now in Blue Springs—"

I didn't hear the rest of it. In the city I had been struck by the lavish spending of money, money which was at such a premium out here. There was something shockingly disproportionate in the capacity to spend by city people and those on farms.

"At least, the crops look good."

"But," Ida Mary pointed out, "they need rain, and the dams are beginning to get low."

"What about the wells the settlers are digging for water supply?"

"They get nothing but dry holes," she told me. "Some of the settlers brought in well-drills, but they didn't find water. They don't know what to do."

All other issues faded into the background before the urgency of the water problem. I packed my city clothes deep down in the trunk, never to be worn again, and went to work!

A casual glance revealed no sign of the emergency we were facing. The Lower Brulé was a broad expanse of green grass and grain, rippling gently in the breeze like water on a quiet sea. Sufficient moisture from the snow and early rain had been retained in the subsoil for vegetation. But we needed water. With the hot weather the dams were going dry. There had been increased demands for water this summer, and there had not been the late torrential rains to fill the dams as there had been the year before.

"What are we going to do?" I asked the other settlers.

"Haul water until we can get wells. We'll have to dig deeper. Perhaps we have just not struck the water veins. After this we will follow the draws."

Water-hauling again! But haul it from where? There was no supply in the country sufficient for the needs of the region. Drills would cost money, and few settlers had any money left. There was no sign of rain, and an oppression weighed upon everyone as of impending evil—the fear of a water famine.

First we had come to understand the primitive worship of fire. Now we began to know that water is as vital to life as air itself. It takes experience to bring home the meaning of familiar words.

In the meantime the tall waving crops brought land agents with their buyers. At the first sign of water shortage more claims were offered for sale, and by that time there were a few deeded tracts put on the market. Loan agents camped at the settlement, following up settlers ready to prove up. One could borrow more than a thousand dollars on a homestead now.

The money coming through our hands on relinquishments, options, government payments, etc., was mainly in bulk and growing beyond the coffee cans and old shoes where we secreted money awaiting deposit at the bank. We did need a bank on the Brulé.

During the long hot summer weeks, when it did not grow dark on the open plain until far into the night, a great deal of traveling was done at night. It was easier for man and horse. On moonlight nights that white light shining through the thin atmosphere made the prairie as light as day, but ghostly; moonlight softened the contours of the plains and robbed them of their color; sounds traveled great distances, seeming to come from space; the howling of coyotes down the draw, the shrill, busy sound of insects in the long grass, the stamping of the horses in the barn, accentuated the stillness; they did not break it. Even the prairie wind came softly, sweet with the scent of hay, not lifting its voice on those hushed nights.

With the stillness invading one's flesh and bones, and the prairie, washed by moonlight, stretching out beyond one's imagination, I wondered that I had ever feared space and quiet.

But out of the silence would come the rhythmic thud of a horse's feet and a loud hail. The Ammons settlement was a day-and-night institution. With a loud knock on the door would come the identification, "It's Alberts!" Or Kimball, or Pinchot—real estate agents. "I've got a man here who wants to pay a deposit on N.W. quarter of section 18. We're on our way to the Land Office. Want to be there when it opens."

One of us would light the print-shop lamp, make out the papers, take the money, and stumble back to bed. A sign, "Closed," or "Never Closed," would have been equally ineffective in stopping the night movement on the Strip. Homesteaders living miles away came after the long day's work to put in their proving-up notices. They must be in the paper the following day to go through the five weeks' publication before the date set at the Land Office. During those scorching weeks their days were taken up by hauling water and caring for things at home.

With those urgent night calls we did not stick a gun out as had the Presho banker. We were not greatly perturbed about the possibility of anyone robbing us. A burglar who could find the money would accomplish more than we could do half the time, so outlandish had the hiding places become. Imbert insisted that we keep a loaded gun or two on the place, but we knew nothing about handling guns and were more afraid of them than of being molested.

Ada put up her folding cot at night in the lean-to kitchen, and one day she brought a rawhide whip from home and laid it on the 2 × 4 scantling that girded the walls—"the two-be-four" she called it. "You don't need a gun," she said in her slow, calm voice. "Just give me a rawhide." With that sure strong arm of hers and the keen whip, one would never enter without shooting first.

143

There were a few nights when we woke to find Ada standing still as a statue in her long white cotton nightgown, straw-colored braids hanging down her back, rawhide in her right hand, only to find who-ever had prowled around had driven on, or that it was Tim Carter, the lawyer, coming home from town intoxicated, talking and singing at the top of his voice.

During that clock-round period the days were usually quiet and we worked in shifts as much as our many duties permitted. "Come on, girls," Ma would call, "this ice tea is goin' to be hot if you don't come and drink it. Now this isn't made from dam water. Fred hauled it over from the crick. (Fred Farraday did things like that without mentioning them.) It's set in the cave all day. Now the Ladies' Aid back in Blue Springs sticks a piece of lemon on the glass to squeeze in—just to get your fingers all stuck up with. I never was one for mixing drinks."

Ma poured an extra glass for Van Leshout, who had just come in with letters to mail. "Tomorrow we'll have the lemonade separate. Come on, Heine, don't you want a glass of tea?"

"Naw." Offering Heine tea was the one thing that shook his calm-ness.

"You don't expect he-men like Heine to drink tea," protested Van Leshout. A sly grin on Heine's face which the artist quickly caught on paper.

"Pa drinks it," from Ma, with that snapping of the jaw which in Ma expressed emphasis. Poor old Pa was the shining example of mas-culinity in her eyes.

Like a sudden breath the hot winds came. The dams were getting dangerously low. The water was dirty and green-scummed and thick. And Ada's folks lost a horse and a cow—alkalied.

The drier it became the whiter the ground on the alkali spots. We had no alkali on the great, grassy Brulé, but there were strips outside the reservation thick with it, and the water in those sections contained enough of it to turn one's stomach into stone.

Carrying the mail from the stage, I saw along the trail horses and cattle leaning against the fences, or lying down, fairly eaten up with it, mere skin and bones; mane and tail all fallen out, hoofs dropped off.

A number of settlers had not a horse left that could put his foot to the ground to travel. Every day there were a few more horses and cows lying dead over the pastures. Gradually, however, most of the afflicted stock picked up, got new hoofs, new manes and tails.

The livestock, even the dogs and the wild animals on the plains, drank from little holes of reservoirs at the foot of the slopes until the water became so hot and ill-smelling that they turned away from it.

But the settlers skimmed back the thick green scum, dipped up the water, let it settle, and used it. The dam water must be boiled, we warned each other, yet we did not always wait for a drink of water until it had been boiled and cooled. Late that summer, when the drying winds parched the country, the dams became the only green spots left on the yellow plains. But the cry for rain was no longer for the fields, it was for the people themselves.

A few narrow, crooked creeks cut their way through the great tableland of prairie. But they were as problematic as the Arkansas Traveler's roof in that they overflowed in the rainy season when we did not need water, and were dry as a bone when we did need it. The creeks were dry now—except the water holes in the creek beds and a few seep wells which homesteaders living near the creeks had dug and into which water from the creeks had seeped.

Proving-up time came for a few, and the ones who had not come to farm left as soon as they proved up—at least until the following year. And the situation was so serious we were glad to have them go— the fewer there were of us the less water we would need.

To add to the troubles of the homesteaders, there were increased activities by claim jumpers. Almost equal to the old cattle-rustling gangs were the land rustlers who "covered up" land as the cattle thieves did brands, making mavericks out of branded stock. Technicalities, false filings, or open crookedness were used to hold rich valleys and creeks and water holes open—or to block the settler's proof title.

Because the problem was a federal one, the courts and men like Judge Bartine were powerless to act in the matter. The West needed fearless representation in Washington. If John Bartine were elected, westerners said, he would fight the land graft. "But there must be a strong campaign against it on the ground," he emphasized. "The frontier newspapers can become the most powerful agency in abolishing this evil."

"Could *The Wand* help?" I asked.

"Its influence not only would be effective," he assured me, "but it would set a precedent and give courage to other little proof sheets."

So *The Wand* took up the issue, using what influence it had to bring a halt to the activities of the claim jumpers. And the homesteaders continued their battle for the thirsty land. Whisky barrels and milk cans were the artillery most essential to keep this valiant army from going down in defeat. They were as scarce as hen's teeth and soared sky high in price, so great was the demand on the frontier. Barrel and can manufacturers must have made fortunes during the years of water-hauling in the homestead country.

The size of a man's herd, and thus his rank as a farmer, was judged by the number of barrels and cans surrounding his shack or barn.

Ida Mary bought a barrel and several new milk cans. "You cannot use the barrel for water," Joe Two-Hawk said. "It is yet wet with fire-water." He drained a pint or more of whisky from it. It would have to be burned out. No one wanted fire-water these days.

Across the hot stretches, from every direction, there moved processions of livestock being driven to water; stone-boats (boards nailed across two runners), with barrels bobbing up and down on them, buggies, wagons, all loaded with cans and barrels.

Ida Mary and I led our livestock to a water hole three miles away, filling water cans for ourselves. The Ammons caravan moving across the hot, dry plain was a sorry spectacle, with Ida in the vanguard astride old Pinto, her hair twisted up under a big straw hat. Lakota insisted upon jumping the creek bed, and we were not trained to riding to hounds. In the flank, the brown team and Lakota, the menagerie following behind. Coming up from the rear, I sat in the One-Hoss Shay behind Crazy Weed, the blind and locoed mare, with the water cans rattling in the back end of the buggy. I too wore an old straw hat, big as a ten-gallon sombrero, pushed back on my head to protect my sunburnt neck, and an old rag of a dress hanging loose on my small body, which was becoming thinner.

The sun blazed down on the shadeless prairie, and the very air smelled of heat. The grain was shriveled and burnt. And for shelter from that vast furnace, a tar-paper shack with a low roof.

As we reached the creek, Crazy Weed, smelling water, leaped to the creek bed, breaking the tugs as she went, leaving the horseless buggy, the empty cans and me high and dry on the bank.

We patched up the tugs, fastened them to the singletree with hairpins, hitched up Pinto, drove down to the water hole and filled our cans.

When we got back to the settlement we saw Lone Star on Black Indian, waiting for us. He dismounted, threw the reins to the ground and carried the water cans into the cool cave.

"Don't know what we're goin' to do with the range stock," he said anxiously, "with the grass dried up and the creeks and water holes on the range goin' dry."

"Lone Star," I said, "don't you think it's going to rain soon?"

Yesterday I had asked Porcupine Bear, and he had shaken his head and held up one finger after another, counting off the moons before rain would come.

"What will become of the settlers?" asked Ida Mary.

"The quicker these homesteadin' herds vacate," Lone Star answered in that slow drawl of his, "the better for everybody. The hot winds have come too early. Goin' to burn the pastures, looks like; hard to find water now for the cattle."

He handed us two flasks of cold water. "Brought 'em from the river; filled 'em while the water was cold early this morning."

Cold, clear water! We drank great long draughts of it, washed ourselves clean and fresh in a basin half-full of water.

One day Tim Carter came by sober. "The damn homestead is too dry for a man to drink water, say nothing of whisky," he stormed. "I'm going to have water if it takes my last dollar."

He brought in a drill. For several days neighbors helped with the drilling; others flocked around with strained anxiety, waiting, waiting for that drill to strike water.

Then one scorching afternoon the drillers gave a whoop as they brought up the drill. "Oil! Oil! There's oil on this drill. Damned if we ain't struck oil!"

Tim Carter's straight, portly figure drooped. He put his hands in his pockets, staring aghast at the evidence before him. "Oil!" he shouted. "Who in hell wants oil? Nobody but Rockefeller. It's water we want!"

"Pack up your rig, boys," he said in a tone of defeat, as though he'd made a final plea in court and lost the case. A discouraged, disheartened group, they turned away.

Thirst became an obsession with us all, men and animals alike. Cattle, breaking out of pastures, went bawling over the plains; horses went running wildly in search of water. People were famished for a cold drink.

"I don't believe we ought to drink that water," I heard Ida Mary tell Ma Wagor, as she stood, dipper in hand, looking dubiously into the bucket.

"Oh, never mind about the germs," Ma said. "Just pick out them you see and them you can't see oughtn't hurt anybody. You can't be persnickety these days." With all that we could see in the water, it did seem as though the invisible ones couldn't do much harm.

With the perverseness of nature, the less water one has the thirstier one becomes. When it is on tap one doesn't think of it. But down to the last half-gallon, our thirst was unquenchable.

The store's supply of salmon and dried beef went begging, while it kept a team busy hauling canned tomatoes, sauerkraut, vinegar. People could not afford lemons, so vinegar and soda were used to make a refreshing, thirst-quenching drink.

Homesteaders reached the point where the whole family washed in the same quart of water. A little more soap and elbow grease, the women said, was the secret. Most of the water used for household purposes did double or triple duty. The water drained from potatoes was next used to wash one's face or hands or dishes; then it went into the scrub bucket. Potato water kept one's hands and face soft, we boasted; it was as effective as face cream.

But I was not a tea-cup saver by nature. Could the time and scheming of those pioneer women to save water have been utilized in some water project, it would have watered the whole frontier. But gradually we were becoming listless, shiftless. We were in a stage of endurance in which there was no point in forging ahead. We merely sat and waited—for rain or wells or whatever might come.

And always when we were down to the last drop, someone would bring us water. I never knew it to fail. One such time we looked up to see Huey Dunn coming. He had made the long trip just to bring us water—two whole barrels of it, although we had not seen him since he moved us to the reservation.

It was so hot he waited until evening to go back. He was in no hurry to return: it was too hot to work. But when had Huey ever been in a hurry? We sat in the shade of the shack, talking. He had dug a well, and his method of fall plowing—fallowing he called it—had proved successful.

Starting home toward evening, he called back, "If you girls take a notion to leave, you needn't send for me to move you—not until you get your deed, anyhow." I only saw him once after that—Ida Mary never again.

Ida Mary was seeing a lot of a young easterner that summer, an attractive, cultured boy who had taken a claim because he had won it in a lottery and it was an adventure. Imbert Miller had gone into the land business. He was well fitted for the work, with his honest, open manner, which inspired confidence in landseekers, and his deep-rooted knowledge of the West.

One day I looked up from my work with a belated thought.

"Imbert hasn't been here for some time. What's the matter?"

"He is to stay away until I send him word. I've got to be sure."

When there was any time for day-dreaming those days I conjured up pictures of snow banks and fountains and blessed, cooling rain, and long, icy drinks of water. The water had alkali in it and tasted soapy in cooking. But it was water. And we drank it gratefully.

The old man from the Oklahoma Run came over. Stooped and stiff, he leaned on his cane in the midst of a group of settlers who had met to discuss the drought and the water problem.

"Now, down in Oklahomy," he began, "it was hotter than brimstone and the Sooners didn't draw ice water from faucets when they settled there." Sooners, we took it, were those who got on the land sooner than the others. "Water was imported in barrels. Buying water was like buying champagne and worse to drink than cawn liquor."

"What did they do?"

"Well, suh," he went on, the long mustache twitching, "one of the fellahs down there was a water witch. He pointed out where the water could be got. Divining rods. That's the solution for the Strip."

But finding expert water witches was almost as difficult as finding water. They had to be imported from some remote section of the West. The witches, as we called them, went over various parts of the reservation, probing, poking, with their forked sticks.

The divining rod was a simple means of locating water, and it had been in common use through the ages, especially in arid regions. It was used in some instances to locate other underground deposits. These rods were pronged branches, sometimes of willow, but preferably of witch-hazel or wild cherry.

If there were water close to the surface, the divining rod would bend and turn with such force that it was hard to keep the prongs in hand. It was said to work by a process of natural attraction, and was formerly regarded as witchcraft or black magic.

Our divining rods refused to twist or bend. If there were water on the Strip, the witches missed it; either that, or it was too deep for the rods to detect. One of the experts said there was indication of some kind of liquid deposit far underground.

The settlers shook their heads and said there must be something wrong with the witches or the divining rod, and Ma Wagor declared, "I never did have any faith in them little sticks."

The hot winds swept the plains like blasts from a furnace. There was not a shelter as far as the eye could see except those little hot-boxes in which we lived. As the sun, like a great ball of fire, lowered to the horizon, a caravan topped the ridge from the north and moved slowly south across the strip. A wagon and a wobble-wheeled buggy, its dry spokes rattling like castanets, went by. Following behind were the few head of stock—horses whinnying, cows bawling, for water. A panting dog, tongue hanging out, trotted beside the wagon. They were shipping out. The railroads were taking emigrants back to the state line free.

Leaving a land of plenty—plenty of everything but water.

A number of homesteaders who had come to stay were getting out. Settlers were proving up as fast as they could. They wanted to prove up while they could get loans on the land. Loan agencies that had vied with one another for the business were closing down on some areas. Despite the water famine, the Brulé had built such prestige, had made such a record of progress, that it was still holding the business. Western bankers kept their faith in it, but the lids of the eastern money-pots, which were the source of borrowing power, might be clamped down any day.

The railroads were taking people back to the state line free, if they wished to go. It seemed to me, exhausted as I was, that I could not go on under these conditions, that the settlers themselves could not go on without some respite.

I walked into the Land Office at Pierre and threw a sheaf of proof notices on the Register's desk. He looked at them with practiced eyes. "These haven't been published yet," he said.

"I don't want them. I'm leaving the country. I came to get nine months' leave of absence for myself and all those whose time is not up. That would give us until next spring to come back and get our deeds."

He leaned over his desk. "Don't pull up and leave at this critical time, Edith," he said earnestly. "There are the legal notices, the loans, the post office—we have depended on you so much, it would be putting a wrench in the machinery out there."

He looked at me for a moment. "Don't start an emigration movement like that," he warned me.

I was dumfounded at his solemnity, at the responsibility he was putting upon me. It was my first realization of the fact that *The Wand* had indeed become the voice of the Brulé; that where it led, people would follow. If my going would start a general exodus, I had to stay.

I walked wearily out of the Land Office, leaving the proofs on his desk. It seemed to me that I had endured all I could, and here was this new sense of community responsibility weighing on me!

A young settler drove me home, and I sat bleakly beside him. It was late when we got near my claim, and the settlement looked dark and deserted. Suddenly I screamed, startling the horses, and leaped from the wagon as there was a loud crash. The heavy timbers of the cave back of the store had fallen in.

I shouted for Ida Mary, and there was no answer from the shack or the store. If she were under that wreckage.... Frantically we clawed at the timbers, clearing a space, looking for a slip of a girl with long auburn braids of hair. It was too dark to see clearly, and in my terror I was ripping the boards in any fashion while Jack strove to quiet me.

"What's the matter?" said a drowsy voice from the door of the shack. It was Ida Mary, who had slept so heavily she had not heard our arrival or our shouts or the crash of the cave-in.

I ran to her, sobbing with relief. "The cave's fallen in. I thought maybe you were in it."

She blinked sleepily and tried to comfort me. "I'm all right, sis," she said reassuringly. "It must have gone down after I went to bed. Too much sod piled on top, I guess. Now we'll have to have that fixed."

As I lay in bed, shaking with fatigue and nerve tension, Ida mumbled drowsily, "Oh, the fresh butter Ma brought me is down in that cave." And she fell asleep. A few moments later I too was sleeping quietly.

The nights were the life-savers. The evening, in which the air cooled first in the draws, then lifted softly to the tableland, cooling the body, quenching the thirst as one breathed it deeply. The fresh peaceful night. The early dawn which like a rejuvenating tonic gave one new hope. Thus we got our second wind for each day's bout.

The next day the proof notices I had turned in to the Land Office came back to me without comment. I explained to Ida Mary what I had done. "I told him we were going back, and he said I must not start an emigration movement. I applied for leaves of absence while the railroads are taking people to the state line free."

"And what," inquired Ida Mary dryly, "will they do at the state line? Go back to the wife's kinfolk, I suppose."

She was right, of course. I began to see what this trek back en masse would mean. What if the land horde went marching back? Tens of thousands of them milling about, homeless, penniless, jobless. Many of them had been in that position when they had stampeded the frontier, looking to the land for security. With these broad areas deserted, what would become of the trade and business; of the new railroads and other developments just beginning their expansion?

We were harder hit than most districts by the lack of water, but if that obstacle could be solved the Brulé had other things in its favor. The words of the Register came back to me: "Don't start an emigration movement."

The Wand came out with an editorial called, "Beyond the State Line, What?" It was based on Ida Mary's terse comment, "Back to the wife's kinfolk," and concluded with my own views of the economic disaster which such a general exodus would cause.

It took hold. Settlers who were ready to close their shacks behind them paused to look ahead—beyond the state line. And they discovered that their best chance was to fight it out where they were—if only they could be shown how to get water.

No trees. No shade. Hot winds sweeping as though from a furnace. And what water one had so hot and stale that it could not quench thirst.

We could ask our neighbors to share their last loaf of bread, but it was a bold, selfish act to ask for water. I have seen a gallon bucket of drinking water going down; have seen it get to the last pint; have held the hot liquid in my mouth as long as possible before swallowing it.

The distances to water were so long that many times we found it impossible, with all the work we had on hand, to make the trip; so we would save every drop we could, not daring to cook anything which required water.

One of the girl homesteaders came over with an incredible tale to tell. She had visited one of the settlers outside the reservation gate who had a real well. And his wife had rinsed the dishes when she washed them.

Ma prophesied that she would suffer for that.

Heine said one day, "My Pa don't wanta leave. We ain't got no moneys to take us, Pa says."

There were many families in the same position. Get out? Where? How?

One day when Chris Christopherson came in I asked him why he thought the water supply would be better in a year or so.

"We can dig better dams. If they bane twice so big this year, they be full now from the snows and rains. We would yet have water plenty."

"We could dig cisterns, couldn't we?"

"Cost money, but not so much like deep wells. Trouble bane we not have money yet nor time to make ready so many t'ings."

"Some of the farmers say," I told him, "that when we cultivate large areas, loosening the soil for moisture absorption, they will be able to get surface wells, especially in the draws. They say the tall, heavy grass absorbs the surface and underground water."

Chris nodded thoughtfully. "Water will be more comin' in time," he declared. "The more land plowed, the more moisture will go down in the soil. It all the time costs more money to move and settle yet than to stay where you are. And nobody knows what he find somewhere else again."

And we got thirstier and thirstier. "I've got to have a drink," I would wail.

"You'll get over it," Ma would assure me.

But we did not always get over it. I remember trying to go to bed without a drink one night and thinking I could not stand it until morning. In the middle of the night I woke Ida Mary.

"I'm so thirsty I can't stand it any longer."

"Let's hitch up and go for some water."

So off we went in the middle of the night, driving over to McClure, where we drank long and long at the watering troughs.

With few water holes left, some of the settlers went over the border, hauling water from outside—from McClure, even from Presho, when they went to town. Somehow they got enough to keep them from perishing.

Men cleaned out their dams "in case it should rain." But there was no sign of the drought breaking. Except for the early matured crops, the fields were burned; the later crops were dwarfed. Our spirits fell as we looked at our big field of flax which had given such promise. Seed which had had no rain lay in the ground unsprouted. Some of the farmers turned their surplus stock loose to forage for themselves.

Public-spirited men like Senator Scotty Phillips and Ben Smith, a well-to-do rancher living four miles from the settlement, dug down into the bowels of the earth for water. Ben Smith went down 1200 feet. There was no sign of water. Despondency gripped the people. "You can dig clear to hell and you won't find water," one of them declared.

"All right, boys," Ben Smith told them, "dig to hell if you have to, and don't mind the cost." Slowly the drill bored on down the dry hole. Ben Smith's Folly, they called it.

The Wand urged the people to put their resources together— water, food, everything—so that they might keep going until water was found or until—it rained. Today pooling is a common method of farm marketing. We have great wheat pools, milk pools, and many others. At that time there were cooperative pools in a few places, although I had never heard of one, nor of a farm organization. But it was the pooling system that was needed to carry on.

Of one thing there was no doubt. The grass on the Indian lands *was* greener than the grass on the settlers' lands. Through their land ran the Missouri River, and they had water to spare. While the homesteaders were famishing and their stock dying for water, it was going to waste in Indian territory. That area was as peaceful as though the whole frontier were filled with clear, cool streams.

So Ida Mary and I went to the Indians for help. I presume we should have gone to the Agency, but we had never seen the government officials in charge, and we did know our Indians.

We rode over into the little Indian settlement. Rows of buffalo-hide and canvas wigwams; Indians sitting around on the ground. Men whittling, doing beadwork, or lounging at ease. Squaws sitting like mummies or cooking over open fires for which they broke or chopped wood. Young bucks riding about, horses grazing peacefully, mongrel dogs in profusion. Children, dirty, unconcerned, playing in the sun. Rows of meat, fly-covered, drying on the lines.

They were peaceful and unconcerned; the whole settlement had about it the air of being on a holiday, the lazy aftermath of a holiday. Remembering the hard labor, the anxiety, the effort and strain and despair in the white settlement, there was a good deal to be said for this life, effortless, without responsibility, sprawling in the shade while others did the work.

It was not before these members of the tribe, however, that we presented our request. We went before the chief and his council with form and ceremony. The old chief, dressed in dignified splendor, sat on a stool in front of his wigwam, a rich Navajo rug under his feet. He had been a great leader, wise and shrewd in making negotiations for his tribe. He looked at me and grunted.

I explained at length that I had come to him from the Brulé white men for help. But I got no farther. He threw out his hand in a negative gesture. The old warriors of the council were resentful, obstinate. They muttered and shook their heads angrily. No favors to the whites who had robbed them of their lands!

I sat down beside the chief while I talked to him, and then to other members of the council—to Porcupine Bear, Little Thunder, Night Pipe. The Indian demands pomp and ceremony in the transaction of affairs. These wanted to hold a powwow. But I had no time for ceremony.

The Indians had *minne-cha-lu-za* (swift-running water). We had none. If some of the settlers could run stock on their hunting ground where they could get to water, and if we could have water hauled from their lands, we would pay.

The old chief sat as immobile and dignified as a king in court. We soon learned that the Indian horse-and-bead traders are a different species from the high powers of the tribe sitting in council, making treaties. It was like appearing before a high tribunal.

"Take Indian lands. All time more," grunted one of them.

"The settlers' land is no good to the Indian," I argued; "no water, no berries, no wood, no more value. The government is making the whites pay money, not giving them allotments as they do the red men."

If they would not give us *minne-cha-lu-za*, I went on, we could not print the paper any more, or keep *she-la*, or trade for posts.

They went into ceremonious council, and delivered their concession officially by an interpreter, Little Thunder I think it was, attired in all his regalia of headdress with eagle feathers, beaded coat, and fringed breeches.

It appealed to their sense of power to grant the favor. At last the whites had to come to them for help. Whether the deal was official or unofficial, no one cared. In those crucial days Washington seemed to the homesteaders as remote as the golden gates.

We took a short-cut back. There was not a single building anywhere in sight, and the only moving thing was a herd of range cattle going slowly toward water. Through the silence came a deep, moaning sound, the most eerie, distressed sound I ever heard. I was passing an Indian cemetery, and beside a grave stood an Indian woman—alone with her dead.

As is the Indian custom, she had come alone, walking many miles across the plain. She would probably slash her breast or mutilate her flesh in some other way as a sacrament to her grief. As I rode on slowly, her wailing cry rose and fell until it grew dim in my ears, blending with the moaning sound of the wind.

155

Some of the settlers turned stock over on the Indian lands after our negotiations, and the Indians hauled loads of life-giving water to the print shop now and then. Our collection of antique animals we turned loose to go back and live off the Indians.

"Might be it will rain," Heine said one day. "Did you see that cloud come by in front of the moon last night?"

But it wasn't a cloud. It was smoke.

XIV. THE LAND OF THE BURNT THIGH

We were living in the Land of the Burnt Thigh, the famous hunting ground of the Brulé Indians, whose name was derived from a great prairie fire which had once swept the land.

The story of that great fire was told me by a famous interpreter who had heard the tale many times from his grandfather. It was three seasons after the big flood of 1812, he said, and the grass was high on Bad River, bringing many buffalo down from the north. About two weeks after the leaves turned they went to the prairie to get the winter's meat. Being a hunting party, the women and children accompanied them. The young boys wandered from the camps, shooting prairie dogs and small birds. One day when a number of boys were returning to camp, a great prairie fire swept down from the north.

The boys ran for the river, but the fire was too swift for them, and they were overtaken. Throwing themselves on the ground, they turned their faces from the fire and wrapped their heads and bodies in their robes, waiting for the fire to pass. Where they lay the grass was high and there were many small bushes; so when the fire came, the ground was hot and they were all burned on the right thigh, though otherwise unhurt.

The escape of the boys was considered so remarkable that the Sioux called this tribe the "people with the burnt thigh." Apparently some French trader rendered the name into his language, and thus we have "Brulé" or burned.

The Land of the Burnt Thigh was famous not only for its great prairie fire and the fact that it had been the feeding ground of the buffalo, which had come in big herds to winter pasture; but also because it had been a notorious rendezvous for horse thieves. In the early days lawless gangs turned to stealing horses instead of robbing banks. A bold outfit of horse thieves plied their trade over a vast section of the Bad River country, of which the Brulé had been a part. Here in the tall grass they found refuge and feed for the horses, with water in the creeks and water holes almost the year around. In the night they would drive their loot in, and the law was helpless in dealing with them.

Much has been said of Indians stealing the white man's horses and little of the depredations of the whites upon the Indians. These gangs stole constantly from the Indians, taking the best of their herds. A little band of Indians, realizing that they must get back their horses at any cost, tracked the thieves and here on the Burnt Thigh attacked them. But they were driven back by the outlaws, who had their lookout, according to the Indians, on the very site of Ammons; concealing themselves here in the tall grass, they could see anyone approaching for miles around. They had seen the Indians coming, just as we had seen them that first day at the settlement. The gang opened fire, killed several of their number, and routed the rest.

The Indians made no protest. All they knew of law was the power of the government, a force not to be appealed to for protection, but rather one against which the red men must struggle for their rights. They had no recourse, therefore, against the thieves. And it was not until the National Guard was sent to round them up that this lawless band was tracked to its lair and captured.

On the Land of the Burnt Thigh that summer the grass was dry, and nowhere was there water with which to fight fire. Heat waves like vapor came up from the hard, dry earth. One could see them white-hot as they rose from the parched ground like thin smoke. From the heat expansion and the sudden contraction when the cool of the night came on, the earth cracked open in great crevices like wide, thirsty mouths, into which horses stumbled and fell beneath their riders.

A young couple went to town one day and returned that night, looking for their home. They wandered around their claim, seeking their shack. It lay in ashes, destroyed by a prairie fire.

Heine came wading through the hot yellow grass. "Did you carry matches with you, Heine?"

"Nope," he answered laconically. "I don't need no matches."

"Suppose a prairie fire should come?" Everyone was supposed to carry matches; no child was allowed to leave home without matches and instructions to back-fire if he saw a fire coming. Heine sat down and wiped the sweat from his face with the sleeve of his little shirt.

"I look first behind when I start. Can't no prairie fire come till I get here."

"But with these hot winds—"

We watched constantly for the first sign of smoke. Sacks, old heavy comforts and pieces of carpet were kept at hand as fire extinguishers, in case there were enough water on hand to wet them—which was seldom.

There were no more water holes, and it got dryer and hotter. Ben Smith's men were still drilling for water. They were down 1500 feet. From the print shop we could hear the drill grinding through hard earth.

Prairie fires began to break out all around the Strip. The homesteaders began to be afraid to leave their shacks for fear they would find them gone on their return. Ammunition for the fight was pitifully meager. They fought with plows that turned firebreaks, back-fired to stop the progress of the fire, beat it out with their wet sacks.

If fire ever got a start on the Burnt Thigh now, with its thick high grass as dry as powder and no water, every habitation would be completely annihilated. Protests about our lack of protection seethed until they found expression in the newspaper. We had no equipment, no fire fighters, no lookouts, no rangers. Surely the government owed us some means of fighting the red devil of the plains.

One evening when the parched ground was beginning to cool we noticed a strange yellow haze settling over the earth, felt a murky heat.

The world was on fire! Not near the settlement, miles away it must be, probably on the Indian lands beyond the Strip.

From the heat in the air, the threatening stillness, the alertness of the animals as they lifted their heads high in the air with nostrils dilated, we knew it was coming toward us. The heavy reddish fog portended a big fire, its tongue of flame lapping up everything as it came.

Already a group of homesteaders was gathering at the print shop, organizing systematic action; men from every section hurrying in with little sacks and kegs of water splashing until they were half empty; a pathetic, inadequate defense to set up against so gigantic an enemy. Chris Christopherson rattled by with his tractor to turn broad furrows. Dave Dykstra, who would never set the world on fire but would do a good deal in putting it out, hastened up to help. Here they came! Men with kegs of water, men with pieces of carpet, men with nothing but their hands and their fear to pit against the fire.

Off to the south the sky was red now, and the smell of fire was in our nostrils, faint but unmistakable. None of us knew how fast a big fire could travel. The settlers still knew so pitiably little about combating the frontier.

From the Indian settlement came Swift Running Deer on the horse which had taken the State Fair prize last year. In Sioux (the young buck was too excited to remember his English) he said the fire was on beyond the Brulé somewhere. Most of the Indians had ridden off to it while he had come to tell the whites.

"If the wind stay down, it mebbe no come, but heap big fire like that take two day—three day—mebbe seven to die."

It was still and peaceful now, but there was little hope that two or three days could pass without wind—and if the wind came from that direction there was no hope for the Brulé.

Coyote Cal, who had come riding through the Strip, stopped at the print shop. Ida Mary tried to persuade him to ride around to the homesteads and tell the girls who lived alone that the fire was still a long way off and that men had gone to fight it.

Coyote Cal stretched his long, angular figure to full height and stood there hesitant. "No, miss, I'd ruther fight fire," he said at length.

"But the girls will be frantic with fear."

"Hain't no use a calf-bawlin' over a prairie fire. If it gits yuh, it gits yuh, an' that's all there is to it."

With these consoling words he swung into the saddle and turned his horse's head toward the fire.

Ma Wagor came outside where Ida Mary and I watched the reflection of flame against the darkening sky. The air was still. There was no wind.

"I'm goin' home to milk the cow," Ma announced. She had paid forty dollars for that cow, she reminded us, and she wanted every last drop of milk out of her. Besides, she didn't believe in anybody leaving this world hungry.

The red dusk found the plains stirring. The ominous silence was broken by rumbling wagons hurrying with their barrels of water, tractors chugging, turning long fresh rows of dirt as breaks, teams everywhere plowing around shacks and corrals.

Night came on, inky black. The red light on the horizon and billowy clouds of smoke intensified the darkness. Over the range, cattle were bellowing in their mad fear of fire. They were coming closer to the reservation fence, running from danger.

The hours crept past; around us on the plains the settlers had done all they could, and they were waiting as Ida Mary and I were waiting, watching the red glow on the sky, thinking of the men who were desperately beating out the advancing flames, wondering if each tiny gust foretold the coming of the wind.

Inside the shack we moved about restlessly, putting the money we had on hand in tin cans, the legal paper in the little strong box, and burying them in the small, shallow cave. If the fire came, we would seek refuge there ourselves, but it wouldn't be much use. We knew that.

Out again to look at the sky, and then up and down the print shop, restlessly up and down. Ida Mary made coffee; we had to do something, and there was nothing for us to do but wait. Wait and listen to the silence, and look our own fear squarely in the eyes and know it for what it was.

"What's that?" said Ida Mary in a queer, hoarse voice. She put down her cup and sat rigid, listening. Then she jumped to her feet, her face white. "Edith," she cried, "it's the wind—it's the wind!"

Out of nowhere came the moaning sound of the wind, sweeping unchecked across space, blowing from the south! While we listened with caught breath, it seized some papers and sent them rattling across the table, blew a lock of hair in my eyes, made the dry grass rustle so that it sounded for one glorious moment like rain.

We ran outside and stood in the darkness, our dresses whipping around us, looking at the sky. Here and there above the red haze we saw a bright, jagged tongue of flame leap up, licking the black sky.

The homesteaders who had not gone to the fire found waiting alone intolerable, and one by one they drifted in to the store, waiting taut and silent.

At midnight we heard the staccato beats of a horse's hoofs. A messenger was coming. Only one horse on the plains could travel like that; it was Black Indian. And a moment later Lone Star Len flung himself from the horse and came in.

He had been fighting flame. His face was blackened almost beyond recognition.

"It's all right," he said at once, before we could question him. "The fire's over on the government land. It's beyond the Strip."

His eyes and lips were swollen, face and hands blistered. "It's still ragin'," he went on, "but there is a little creek, dry mostly, between the fire and the Strip. It's not likely to get this far. 'Course, the wind is bad. It's blowin' sparks across on the grass, this side of the creek. But some of the settlers and Indians are watchin' it."

Ida Mary came in from the shack with sandwiches and black coffee and set them before him.

"You didn't need to bother doin' that for me," he protested; "you girls better go to bed."

"When did you have anything to eat?" Ida Mary asked, as he drank the hot coffee and devoured the food ravenously, moving his hands as though they hurt him unbearably.

"This mornin'. Been working with that fire since noon; I had started for the chuck-wagon when I smelt smoke...."

"Lone Star, why did you risk your life to save a reservation full of homesteaders?" I asked him.

He stood for a moment with a chagrined expression on his smoke-scarred face.

"Cattle needs the grass," he replied as he stalked out and rode slowly, wearily away into the flame-lighted night.

The fire had broken out on range and government land off toward the White River country—to the southeast, where Lone Star rode herd. As the country for the most part was uninhabited, the fire had swept the plains for miles before the fighters reached it. Sparks and flames had jumped the creek, but by now the grass was burned back far enough on both sides so that the danger for this region was past.

The amused natives told how a man had jolted up on a stiff horse, a painting outfit in his saddlebag, to watch the fire. "This is great," he exclaimed as he plied brush and color. Then, as a volley of wild sparks shot across the narrow stream and went into flame nearby, he threw down the brush, rushed in among the fire-fighters, worked madly until the flames were extinguished, then went back and finished the picture.

"Who is he?" someone in the gaping crowd asked.

"The cartoonist from Milwaukee," a Brulé settler answered.

For several days longer the fire raged, with the air smoky and a red and black pall over the earth. Then it faded as our other terrors had faded, and was gone.

Already, in the midst of fire and water famine, there stalked ghosts of cold and hunger—the coming winter. With no money left to provide the necessities of life, the homesteaders stared into the face of a food famine. Most of them were now living on meager rations, counting every penny, their crops shriveled in the fields.

Ada put her small wages into flour and coffee. And Heine remarked, "My Ma says might be we'll starve and freeze yet. She's goin' to pray." We watched him trudge back across the plains, a sturdy little fellow, one suspender holding up patched overalls over a faded blue shirt, bare feet which walked fearlessly and by some miracle escaped the constant menace of rattlesnakes, ragged straw hat shading the serious round face. The plains had made him old beyond his six years.

With the realization of danger which the prairie fire had brought, *The Wand* began to advocate government rangers and lookouts to be stationed at strategic points. I was in the print shop writing an article on conditions when Lone Star came in.

"I want to get my paper forwarded, Miss Printer," he stated; "I'm leavin' the country. It's gettin' too crowded in these parts. Too lonesome. I don't see how people can live, huddled up with somebody on every quarter-section."

"Where are you going now?"

"Goin' to an honest-to-God range country," he said. "A short-grass country, but rich feed. You can get away from landgrabbers there. It's bigger'n all creation."

"Where shall I send the paper?"

"Wyoming. The Rawhide country. Just send the paper to Lost Trail. I'll be goin' on there. I know a cattleman around Lost Trail."

Rawhide country. Lost Trail. About them was the atmosphere of far-flung space, of solitude and peace.

"I may go there myself some day," I told him.

"If you do," he said soberly, "leave this doggone newspaper she-bang behind. It's a pest to the country. Don't clutter up any more range with homesteadin' herds. Worse than grasshoppers; at least the grass-hoppers leave, and the homesteaders appear to be here to stay."

He rode off, a strange, solitary figure, topped the ridge and dropped out of sight as swiftly as he had appeared that first morning, stopping the eagle in its flight. When he had gone I turned back to my article. In this gigantic homestead project, *The Wand* declared, there should be protection. We demanded of the local land offices why the Department of the Interior did not establish Service Bureaus on government territory to expedite development, to lessen hardship and danger. But the Land Offices could not help us. They were only the red-tape machines of the Public Lands Department.

The federal government was taking in revenue by the millions from the homesteaders. Millions of acres of homestead land at from $1.25 to $6 an acre provided a neat income for the United States Treasury. And, we contended, the homesteaders of America should be given consideration. There was nothing radical about these articles, but here again I became known as "that little outlaw printer."

Had I been experienced, I might have carried this appeal to Washington and said, "Put the revenue from these lands back into them. That is not charity, it is development of natural resources."

Any such entreaty, coming from an upstart of a girl printer, would have been like a lamb bleating at a blizzard. But the homesteaders might have been organized as a unit, with official power to petition for aid. I did not know then that I could do such things.

Meantime the print shop buzzed with activity. The harvest of proofs, on which I had gambled the paper, was on. It kept one person busy with the clerical work on them. While the Strip was yet a no-man's land, I had pledged the printing equipment company 400 proofs as collateral. That was a low estimate. As a matter of fact *The Wand* won an all-time record, publishing in one week 88 proofs, the highest number ever to be published in any issue of a newspaper of which the government had record. From the Department of the Interior, from the Land Office, from other newspapers congratulations poured in. It seems to me that some sort of medal was awarded to us for that.

It wasn't the record which mattered, of course. To us the publication of these notices signified that the settlers had stuck it out with parched throats to get their deeds; that some 14,000 acres of wasteland had passed into private units in one week's time.

It meant endless work. Type, numbers, checking, straining eyes and nerves beyond endurance. But it also meant (for that one lot) over $400 income for the newspaper. Proof money had been coming in for several weeks. Every mail brought long heavy envelopes from the Land Office, containing proof applications made there. From among the homesteaders we hired amateur typesetters to help out, and anybody who happened to be handy turned the press; on occasion we resorted to old Indian warriors, and once to a notorious cattle rustler.

And all this time we watched the sky for rain and skimmed the green scum from the dam water to drink. Looking up from the type one morning, I saw an old Indian standing before me, old Porcupine Bear. Slipping in on moccasined feet, an Indian would appear before one without warning. At first this sudden materializing at my elbow had alarmed me, but I had long grown accustomed to it.

Old Porcupine Bear was a savage-looking character—one of the very old warriors who seldom left camp. One never knew how old some of these aged Indians were, and many of them did not know themselves how many seasons they had lived. This old man, we figured, must be a hundred years old.

"Will there be rain, Porcupine?" I asked him. "Will you hold your Rain Dance soon?"

The deep wrinkles in his leathery face were hard set as if from pain. His coal-black hair, streaked with gray and hanging loose over his shoulders, looked as if it had not been combed for days.

"*To-wea*," he wailed. "*My to-wea* (my woman). Him sick. The fever. Goin' die." He dropped his face into the palm of his hard hand and let it lie there motionless in demonstration of her passing. He wanted to get a box like white squaws had, the boxes in which they went to the Happy Hunting Ground.

He was on the road to Pierre for a coffin. Others of the tribe, we gathered, had put in money to help buy it. He opened a beaded sack and showed us. There was enough to buy a pretty good one. In broken Sioux and signs we advised him to wait—mebbe-no-die. Mebbe-walk-some-more. He shook his head stubbornly. His herbs—he was a medicine man who had healed many sick ones—had not worked. Even his *pazunta* had failed.

The Indian's *pazunta* was his shield against disease—against all evil. It drives the Evil Spirit away. It may be anything he selects—an herb, a stone, a rabbit's foot—so long as he selects it secretly and divulges to no one what it is. The *pazunta* is invested with divine curative power, according to the Indians.

When he got back to his wigwam with the satin-lined "last-sleep-box," Porcupine Bear found his *to-wea* cooking supper; so the old brave, it was said, slept in the good soft bed himself. "Why not?" said

Ida Mary. He had slept on the ground and fought many hard battles; let him have his cushioned resting place while he could enjoy it; but I shuddered at the thought.

A week or so later he came again. It was a day when I was at the breaking point. He stood looking at me, shaking his head as he had done over his *to-wea*. I must have looked like a ghost, for in a gesture of friendship he said:

"You want my last-sleep-box?"

The prairie fire had not got me down, but at the thought of that box I went to bed and stayed there three days.

XV. UP IN SMOKE

There was almost $750 in the tin box down in the trunk ready to be deposited. At breakfast we exulted over it. The Ammons sisters were always draining the bank dry. Sedgwick would open his eyes when we walked into the bank with that bag of money.

We planned to go to Presho that day. It was hardly safe to have so much money in the shack, and we were eager to put it in a safe place. It represented months of planning and effort and hard work. But the labor didn't seem bad to look back on that morning, not with the reward at hand. It had been worth while, because the end of the road was in sight and we had accomplished much that we had hoped to do—more, in some respects.

It was unbearably hot that morning, and we decided against the trip to Presho. After all, one more day wouldn't matter, and the sun was so scorching we quailed at the thought of that long ride. There was an ominous oppression in the air, and heat waves made the ground appear to waver before our eyes. Here and there flames flared up without any explainable origin, as though from the heat of the grass itself.

The day crept on to mid-afternoon, and the hot wind came up from the ground, blistering our faces. There was no one near the print shop, where the metal was hot to the touch, no movement over the plains. We sent our helpers home, while Ma, Ida Mary and I moved about languidly, doing only what was absolutely necessary.

There was a curious, acrid smell in the air. As though a bolt of lightning had struck, I stopped my work on the paper and cried out, "What's that?"

"Fire," screamed Ida Mary; "fire!"

Smoke enveloped us. There was a deafening crackle. Blinding red flame. We ran to the door, and there, not ten feet away, our shack was burning to the ground. The little lean-to kitchen, covered with tar paper, was sending its flames high into the air. Frantically we ran to the front door, shouting above the crackling and roar of flame, "The trunk! The money! The settlers' money!"

The print shop would go, too—and the notices had several weeks to run—but the essential thing was to get the money back. We must do that, must! Oh, for a rolling bank on wheels!

At the front door black smoke came rolling out, choking us. Ida Mary threw a sack over her head and started into the shack. Ma Wagor and I dragged her back into the open air. The building was burning as though it had been made of paper, a torch of orange flames. We watched it go, home, money, clothes, a few valuable keepsakes, furniture—everything we possessed licked up by the flames. The piano, too—I was glad it had brought so much pleasure to the settlers.

The wind! Now the fire was spreading. The print shop was burning, its inflammable tar paper and dry boards blazing like powder. "Hurry, hurry!" we called frantically to each other. From the print shop I grabbed the most valuable papers while Ida Mary snatched what she could from the post office. Stoical, silent, making every move count, Ma Wagor was busy in the store, her store, in which she had taken such pride and such infinite pleasure. Ma was getting more "confusement" now than she had bargained for.

Blinded with smoke, we caught up the sacks into which we had stuffed the papers and threw them into the cave, the only shelter left on the whole claim.

In less than thirty minutes the post office, the store with its supply of food, the print shop were gone. The harvest of long months of labor and storm, thirst and fire, vanished as though it had never been—gone up in clouds of heavy, black smoke.

If the wind would only go down, we groaned; but the sparks had already caught the grass around us. A prairie fire! If it ever jumped those breaks, the Strip would be devastated with the wind sweeping the plain as it was doing. What irony that we who had printed our precautions and warnings for others, should burn up the Strip! We who had labored so to save it! And there was no chance for us. We could not outrun a prairie fire. The horses, which were untied, had gone full speed across the prairie at the first smell and sight of fire.

Now the oilhouse had caught, and we turned, panic-stricken, running headlong across the plains, our feet burning, not knowing where we were going so long as we could escape the explosion of the oil. Inside the firebreaks the grass was burning. Listening for the explosion of the oil was like waiting for the crack of doom. Then we remembered. Pa Wagor had sunk the barrels underground, using siphons, "just in case of fire."

Sparks leaping up, flying across the breaks—the prairie was on fire! We checked our flight, sanity returning with the emergency. We had to go back—simply had to go back and fight that first outbreak of flame. The Strip was at stake. Life and property were at stake. Falling, rising, running, falling again, dragging each other up, we went back. "Help!" we called to the empty prairie, "Help!"

There was nothing to smother the fast-spreading blaze. Not a thing. Not even a sack or a hat. We tore off parts of the clothes from our scantily clad bodies. Ma took off her petticoat. There was a sack in the barn which we wet in a keg set in the yard, wet the canvas which covered the keg. With that, with our feet we trampled down the sparks as they fell, the flames as they rose—shoes hot and charred, holes burning through.

Across the prairie a team was coming at a dead run. "Bless the Lord," Ma Wagor panted, "it's Sam Frye!"

A bright red flare shot up from behind and around me. My dress was on fire. Ida Mary clawed dirt from the hard-baked ground, and with it in her hands twisted my burning smock into knots to keep the flames from spreading. With almost animal instinct I threw myself down in the firebreak, pressing hard against the ground to extinguish any smoldering sparks on my clothing, and lay panting, cooling in the dirt.

Sam Frye, the mail-carrier, was there, taking charge. All at once a crowd had gathered, attracted by the leaping flames on what had been the settlement of Ammons, running to fight the threatening prairie fire. Men went to work, fighting fresh outbursts of flames and putting out fire on the ruins. Women hovered about us in sympathy, some with tears streaming down their sunburned cheeks under the straw hats and bonnets. Neither Sister nor I could shed a tear.

Dazed and dizzy, we stumbled back across the breaks to the charred ashes of our labors. Apart from the tangible losses that lay in coals, the newspaper, the voice of the Brulé, was gone. "Down into frontier history," Senator Phillips said. Into it had gone the ambitions, the heartbreaking labor, the vision of two girls.

Half-naked, our scanty clothing burned and torn, hair singed, faces and parts of our bodies scorched and black with smoke—tar paper makes black, smudgy smoke—eyes red and burning, we stood there in the middle of the open spaces that had dealt us their blow. Our *pazuntas* hadn't worked, that was all. But at least we had checked the prairie fire. We had won that much from the Brulé, the "Burned" land.

We clung to each other wordlessly. There was nothing to say. Everything that made up our daily life and our plans for the future had been wiped out in thirty minutes.

"We still have the claim," Ida Mary murmured at last; "nothing can destroy the land."

"But all our bright hopes—"

How the fire got such a start before we detected it was a mystery. With the shack walls already burning hot and the strong wind, it had been like spontaneous combustion. Ma Wagor was baking bread on an old oil stove. Perhaps a draft from the open window had fanned the fire. But the origin didn't matter now.

Ma Wagor had worked heroically, helping us to save the important records, the mail, and the prairie from being swept by fire. When it was all over she did not whimper about her loss.

When I saw Pa coming, I ran to her. "Ma, here comes Pa. This will kill him. You had better go meet him." He had not wanted her to buy the store in the first place; now there were debts piled up, and only the homestead to pay them.

She sat on the ground, burying her face in her hands. "Let him come to me," she replied. "It's his place to comfort me in time of trouble."

True to her feminine intuition, he went to her and put his arm around her shoulders. "Elizabeth," he said. No response. "Elizabeth," he entreated. "Don't give way like this. We will pull through somehow."

I felt a hand on my arm, and Alex Van Leshout's voice hoarse in my ear. "The latchkey of the Circle V is on the outside. If you girls will come over, I'll move out. If you need me or Hop-Along, all I have is at your service. You're a good Indian, Edith."

Sometimes I envy the women who are able, during a catastrophe, to stop and grieve over it. I never seem to have had the time. There was always something that demanded to be done, whatever the circumstances.

The fire had no sooner been put out, the claim bare as the day I first saw it—save for charred grass, and a great mound of ashes, and the smell of smoke—when Sam Frye opened the mail sacks. Sitting bedraggled in his old buggy, Ida Mary distributed the mail to the patrons who had gathered. Even though the post office was gone, the mail must go on. We were never destined to be back-trailers.

The sultry, tragic day came to a close, with the plains light long after the sun had gone down, and the Ammons settlement gone, and a devastating sense of emptiness. Ida Mary and I realized that we had no place to go. With typical frontier hospitality, every home on the reservation was open to us; but that night we longed to be alone. It wasn't commiseration we needed, but quiet in which to grasp what had happened to us. We decided on Margaret's shack, left vacant when she had proved up. She had left a few household essentials there.

There some of the frontier women followed us, to bathe and salve the burns we had forgotten, bandaging those which were the worst. I had suffered most when my clothing caught fire, but miraculously there were no serious burns.

They left us alone as night came, Ma and Pa Wagor, Ida Mary and me. It was Ma who roused first from the general lethargy in which we were all steeped. She began bustling around. "Guess we'd better have something to eat," she said briskly.

"There's nothing left to eat," Ida Mary reminded her.

Triumphantly, Ma brought forth a big bundle tied up in her old gingham apron. In it were cans of salmon, tomatoes and other essential foods. And a can of pineapple, Ma's panacea for all ills! "I knew we'd be hungry after all that, so I jerked up a little stuff while you were getting the papers out."

She brought in an armful of prairie hay, built a fire in the cookstove and made strong tea. She was no longer the clinging vine of an hour before.

And there in the little shack down the draw, penniless, almost naked, all our belongings and our plans for the future in charred ashes on the claim, we slept from exhaustion.

No matter with what finality things seem to end, there is always a next day and a next. During those first few hours the extent of our disaster had dazed us. Then, the odds seemed so overwhelmingly against us that there was no use in going on. The only trouble was that we couldn't stop. Post office or no post office, there was the mail. Print shop or no print shop, there were the proof notices.

We were like the cowboy who, hanging to a running steer's tail, was dragged against the hard ground and through brush until he was cut, battered and bruised.

Fearing he would be killed, the other cowboys, who watched, shouted wildly to him, "Let go! Let go!"

"Let go, hell!" he yelled back. "It's all I can do to hold on!"

Then there was Great-uncle Jack Ammons, back in the earlier days of Illinois, who had become critically ill from some lingering disease of long standing. One day the doctor called Aunt Jane aside and said, "Jane, if Jack has any business matters to attend to, it had better be done at once. I don't think he can last another forty-eight hours."

From the bedroom came a weak, irritable voice, "Jane! Jane! Where's my boots?"

Uncle Jack got up, fought the disease, and lived and prospered for many a year. We came of a family who died with their boots on.

I don't know whether it was a streak of Great-uncle Jack or whether, like the cowboy, we held on because we could not let go. The latter, perhaps, for we saw no way of escape. Many times, I think, people get too much credit for hanging on to things as a virtue when they are simply following the line of least resistance. We saw no means of escape, and were too stunned to plan.

Of one thing we were sure. We would not go back home for help. There would have to be some way of telling our father of the misfortune so as to soften the blow as much as possible, but we were determined not to add to his burdens, which were already too heavy for him.

"If the railroad company takes us to the state line," declared Ida Mary, "it will have to take us crated—or furnish us covering." In the garish morning light, indeed, we felt rather naked in those flimsy, torn clothes, the only garments we now owned.

"We can't go back, anyhow," I reminded her. "We can't leave things unfinished. The proof notices have to finish running, and Sam Frye will be throwing the mail sack in at the door." It was easier to get into things than to get out.

The settlers came that day with their widow's mite of food and clothes; the women's clothing too large, the children's too small. But it covered us—after a fashion. The store at Presho sent out a box of supplies. Coyote Cal and Sourdough rode up.

"Beats tarnation, now don't it," Coyote Cal consoled us.

"I told you this country wasn't fit for nothin' but cowhands," growled Sourdough. "Here, the punchers rounded up a little chicken feed." He fairly threw at us a dirty tobacco pouch, filled with coins. "Coming before pay day like this, tain't much," he grumbled, as though the catastrophe might have waited for pay day—things couldn't be done to suit Sourdough.

A wagonload of Indians drove up, men and squaws and papooses. They climbed out, unhitched, turned the team loose to graze. They came in mumbling in a sort of long wail, "No-print-paper, hu-uh, hu-uh," but gleeful as children over the gifts they carried. A bright-hued shawl, thick hot blankets, beaded moccasins. There was a sack of "corn in the milk" (roasting ears) which had been raised over by the river, and stripped (dried) meat. We did not know whether it was cow, horse or dog, but we knew it had been black with flies as it hung on the lines drying—we had seen them drying meat. However, parboiling should make it clean.

And early that morning we saw Imbert coming from Presho, hurrying to Ida Mary, his face drawn and haggard. They went into each other's arms without a word, and at last Ida Mary was able to cry, tears of sorrow and relief, with her face against his breast.

I lay weak and ill, wasting from a slow fever. I slept fitfully, while streams of cool water went gurgling by, and cool lemonade, barrels of it. But every time I stooped to take a drink the barrels went rattling across the plain into a prairie fire.

"Maybe you've got typhoid," Ma would say as she bathed my hot head and hands with towels wrung out of vinegar and warm water, fanning them to coolness. "You'll be all right, Sis," Ida Mary would say; "just hold on—" We did not call a doctor. There was no money left for doctors.

Rest, sleep, and nourishment were what I needed, but conditions were far from favorable for such a cure. The deserted shack was baking hot. It was not the cheerful place it had seemed while Margaret lived in it, with the bare floor, the old kitchen stove, the sagging wire couch and a couple of kitchen chairs. We had scanty, sticky food, and warm, sickening water. We didn't even bother to keep it clean. The routine of our life had been burned away. The handful of dishes went dirty, the floor went unswept. But Ma brought milk and custards that she had made at home, I drank the juice of dried fruits, and Imbert brought us water from the Millers' well. We sank jars of it deep into the ground to keep cool.

Heine broke a new trail across the plains and a few days after the fire the horses came home. They had wandered back to the old site, snorted at the black ruins, and gone thundering across the prairie led by Lakota with the wild horse's fear of fire. We never expected to see them again. But one day they saw Sam Frye coming with the mail. They followed him down the draw, and when he stopped and threw out the mail sack Lakota gave a loud neigh and walked straight into Margaret's old barn. Where the mail sacks went was home to Lakota.

Moving the post office around the prairie, piling the mail in an open box in the corner, may have been criminally illegal, but we gave it no thought.

The mail, in a haphazard fashion, was being handled. Our next problem was the proof notices. They must go on. It was vital to the settlers. Many of them could not live without the money they were borrowing on the final proofs. Without the press there seemed no solution to that problem.

On the sixth day after the fire Ida Mary got up early, while I slept in the cool of the morning; she made a blast from the dry grass under one cap of the stove, boiled coffee, ate her lean breakfast, and put food on a chair beside my bed. Then she darkened the room, slipped out, saddled Lakota, rode up to the cave, and brought out the mail sack of legal papers we had saved from the fire. She took out the notices— those in course of publication and others due to be published. Then she rode on to McClure, made arrangements with the printer of the McClure *Press*, and began setting up the notices.

When the stage came in that noon with the Ammons mail, there was a letter from E. L. Senn, the proof king, offering us the use of the shop and part-time service of his printer to meet the emergency. Although we had cornered the great proof business on the Lower Brulé, he was coming to our rescue to save it for us.

That night Ida Mary came home, hot, weary, with lines of fatigue in her youthful face and about her blue eyes. But there was a resolute look, too, marking her strong will; and in her voice a tone of satisfaction.

It was a long, arduous task, setting up again all those notices in small type. The type of the McClure shop would not set half of the notices. We sent the balance of them to be set, some in Presho, some in Pierre, got them back by stage, and *The Wand*, despite fire and all other obstacles, went on with its work—a few days late, strictly a proof sheet, but without lapse of publication.

And Ida Mary kept things going, conserving her strength as well as she could, with Imbert and Ma Wagor helping. Ma said, "I'd 'a' died if I hadn't found something to do."

It was mid-August, with no sign of the drought breaking. In the shack down the draw we sat during spare hours sorting type at Margaret's kitchen table, picking, separating six-point, eight-point, ten-point letters and spaces, leads, slugs. Ma Wagor and other neighbors helped at odd times; Heine separated the type into piles of like sizes. Sorting that type-pi was a job to which no one in the world but a printer can give the deserved sympathy.

Heine, raking around in the cooling embers on my claim, had found several cases of pied type and a few odds and ends of printing equipment down under a piece of heavy tin roofing, the only thing salvaged from the wreckage.

A committee of settlers came, emptied a little sack on the table. In a little heap there lay pennies, dimes, quarters, a few silver dollars—precious coins that had been put aside to keep the wolf from the door—and a separate roll of bills. The offering of the Lower Brulé settlers! "To build a new shack and print shop," they said simply. "The homesteaders will do the building."

Of course, we must build another shack and reestablish residence or there would be no deed to the land. The money represented not only the hard-earned savings but the loyal support of the settlers. When we protested, they laughed. "But *The Wand* has always been telling us to share," they said. Some of the business men of the towns added to the contribution to establish the newspaper.

One sweltering day, with everyone seeking escape from the broiling sun, all movement over the Strip was suspended. As I lay on the couch recuperating, there came a great explosion that roared through the dead hush like all the cannons of war gone off at once. Ida Mary, resting in the shade of the shack, came running in. It could not be thunder, for there was not a cloud in the sky. It had come from over Cedar Fork way.

Soon the plains were astir with settlers rushing in the direction of the explosion. A great rumbling force was sending steam high into the air. It was Ben Smith's Folly. He had struck gas—enough to pipe house and barns for light and fuel!

Then came a heaving, belching from far down in the earth's cavern. And up came the water—a great stream of it that ran over the dry hot ground! Water overflowing. That artesian well, flowing day and night, would save the people and stock until it rained.

And with the flowing of fresh, cool water on the Lower Brulé, life began to flow through my veins once more, and I got up, ready for what was to come.

XVI. FALLOWED LAND

So it happened that only a few weeks before proving-up time, Ida Mary and I had to start all over again. But with the coming of water into that thirsty land it didn't seem so difficult to begin again. And we weren't doing it alone. It was the settlers who built a new shack, a new building for a printing press; the settlers who clothed us during those first destitute days. "This is cooperation," they laughed at our protests. "*The Wand* has always preached cooperation."

In the cool of the evening I rode out over the devastated prairie, past the charred timbers and ashes of my claim, across the scorched and stunted fields blighted by drought, avoiding the great cracks which had opened in the dry earth and lay gaping like thirsty mouths for rain.

The crops were burnt, and the land which had seemed so fertile looked bleak and sterile.

I rode through the reservation gate. There was no one at home at Huey Dunn's, but his little field of shocked grain lay there in the midst of burnt grass and unharvested fields. Instead of dry chaff there were hard, fairly well-filled heads. It had withstood the drought sufficiently to mature. In an average year it would have yielded a good crop.

On his claim near the reservation a young man was doing quite a bit of experimenting. He was a graduate of an agricultural school. I looked at his fields, which also had come through the drought much better than others. From other farmers scattered here and there who had tried the fallowing plan I got records of methods and results. Then I rode back slowly, thinking of what might be done for the Brulé country.

Drinking water supply could be obtained. The next most vital problem was moisture for the crops. Most of the rainfall came in the growing season, but in dry years it was inadequate and much of it wasted on packed ground. To produce crops in the arid or semi-arid regions, out-of-season moisture—heavy snows and rains—must be conserved. There must be a way to harness it.

Next to lack of moisture was the short growing season. These were the principal barriers to converting the new West into an agricultural domain. The latter problem could be solved, the farmers said. Progress already was being made in developing seed adapted to the climate. The Indians had produced quick-maturing corn through their years of corn-raising in a small way. There could be developed a hardier, short-stalked grain, eating up less moisture, agricultural authorities maintained. The farmers said that nature itself gradually would do a great deal toward that end.

Experience. Science. Time. Of course, this was a land of the future, not of today. The homesteaders had expected to tame it in a year or two, when many years must be spent on even the smallest scientific discoveries. They had demanded miracles. That was because they had no resources with which to await results.

President Roosevelt had done much in turning public attention toward the necessity of reclaiming these public lands, and already much was being done. They had been too long neglected. Years ago, when the supply of government land had seemed inexhaustible, the tide of settlers had swept around the forgotten frontier, on beyond the arid and semi-arid land to the fertile soil and the gold fields on the Pacific Coast. But the time had come when this neglected prairie was the only land left for a land-hungry people. Some way had to be found to make the great arid plains productive.

The Department of Agriculture was turning its attention to the frontier, establishing bureaus and experiment stations in various western states, making scientific research.

At the request of *The Wand*, two agricultural agents from the State Experimental Farm came to examine the soil and advise us as to its possibilities, as to crops and cultivation. They reported it rich in natural resources, with splendid subsoil. We would have to depend greatly upon the subsoil and its moisture-retaining quality.

And over the frontier there was talk about a new system of conserving moisture. Some said it was bound to sweep the West. The method was called fallowing—the method Huey Dunn had used. It was a radical departure from anything farmers of the rain belts had ever used.

The few sodbreakers who had tried it thought they had found a way to conserve the moisture and at the same time to preserve the land, but it was not they who heralded the plan as a great new discovery. To them it was a way to raise their own crops. They may have learned it in the Old Country, where intensive farming was carried on, or, like Huey Dunn, figured it out for themselves. But it was ahead of the times in the new West and generally looked upon as an impractical idea spread largely by land agents as propaganda. Many of the farmers had never heard of it. What I had heard and read of fallowing now came back to mind. I was in a position to keep better posted on such things than they.

I got out my letters and records and spread them before Ida Mary on the old square table, and with the sweat dripping down our faces from the heat of the lamp we eagerly devoured their contents. Huey Dunn's plan of mellowing, or rotting the soil, was not yet the true fallowing method.

"But it will mean cropping the land only every other year, and plowing and raking the empty soil," Ida Mary said in a tone of misgiving.

"The top soil is kept loosened so that every bit of moisture will be absorbed into the subsoil. Suppose it does mean letting the land lie idle every other year, alternating the fields," I contended. "There is plenty of cheap land here. It will be a way to utilize waste space." Farmers in other arid regions, I learned as I scanned the letters, were raising forage crops on the land in the off year.

179

But it will take two years, Ida Mary reminded me. The settlers had no money to wait so long for a crop. "And all that labor—" she went on. "It may be the solution, but I doubt if the settlers would listen to any such plan."

I knew she was right. Two years of waiting, labor and expense. Labor was no small item with the poor homesteaders. If the government would put in money to carry out this new system until the farmers could get returns from it—"It is a gigantic project for the government to finance ... it would require great financial corporations to develop this country...." Halbert Donovan had said.

I talked it over with some of the more experienced farmers on the Strip who understood the processes required. They figured they could plant part of the ground while the other lay fallowing. If it happened to be a wet year, that would give them something to go on. "But, mein Gott, how we goin' to pull t'rough next winter?" old man Husmann raved. Even Chris had no answer.

In the years of experimenting, the fallowing system underwent a number of changes. But we had the plan in its fundamentals. After each rain the land should be loosened; and late in the fall it should be plowed rather deeply to soak up the winter snows. The top soil must be kept from packing. It was worth trying, they agreed, if they could get money to pull through this drought and stay on the land.

This might be a solution for the future. But for the people on the land the solution must be immediate. Empty purses could not wait two seasons for a good crop; empty stomachs could not await the future, and famine stared the homesteaders on the Lower Brulé in the face.

Our proof sheet came out with the message, "We Can Fallow!" There was encouragement to be derived from it, of course, but it was hope deferred. Then, sitting in the doorway of the shack, leaning against the jamb for support, my pencil held in tender fingers not yet healed, I wrote to Halbert Donovan, setting forth the possibilities of the Strip, and the West, under a moisture-retaining method of farming.

It was a morning in late August when I turned to see a well-dressed man standing in the open door. Halbert Donovan!

At the first meeting he had found the West green and bright with spring colors, and the outlaw printer of the McClure *Press* excited and voluble over the possibilities of the country. Now the investment broker found a land of desolation and ruin, and the printer in sorry plight, living in a crude, bare shack, clad like some waif of the streets in the clothes donated by the settlers.

But he had come. He had driven out from Pierre along the dusty roads, through the sultry heat, in a long shiny automobile. On the sagging couch leaning against the hot wall, he sat wiping the perspiration from his face as I told him more of the fallowing idea. He had not heard of it. He knew practically nothing about agriculture, but he was a man to whom any method of developing vast resources would appeal.

"At first," he said, little crinkles breaking around his eyes, relieving the sternness of his face, "I read *The Wand* (how I did laugh at the name you gave it) with refreshing amusement, out of a personal curiosity you had aroused. I wanted to see how long you would hold out. Later I became deeply interested in this western activity."

I knew in what mood he must have reached the shack, after that drive from Pierre, across parched earth, seeing the ruined crops, passing settlers' homes which from the outside looked like the miserable huts one sees along waterfronts or in mean outskirts of a city where the flotsam of humanity live. And cluttered around them, farm machinery, washtubs, and all the other junk that could be left outdoors, with countless barrels for hauling water, and the inevitable pile of tin cans. It was dreary, it was unrelievedly ugly; above all, it looked like grim failure.

Earnestly I faced him. "We aren't done," I told him. "We've just begun—badly, I know, but we can fallow. Make reservoirs. Put down artesian wells." I completely forgot, in putting these possibilities of the Strip before him, to mention the gas and oil deposits which we had discovered during our frantic search for water. I did not think of saying, "We have natural gas here—let's go and look at the Ben Smith ranch with all its buildings piped with gas. And over on the Carter place a drill came up from a shallow hole sticky with oil." But the minds of the settlers were so focused elsewhere that little had been said about these things. With an investment broker interested in mining projects under my very roof, many of us might have become rich and the Brulé prosperous in no time.

Development of agriculture, to my mind, was of broader importance than oil strikes, anyhow. "Men do put money into undeveloped things," I said. "Eastern capitalists risk millions in undeveloped mines and oil fields in the West. This is different. Land is solid."

He answered thoughtfully: "As an investment, land is not so precarious as mines, but there are no big profits to be reaped from it. That's the difference, my girl."

He must have known that even for investors, western land was going to be a big thing. He must have known that the railroad companies were buying it up—that the Milwaukee had gone into a spree of land buying in Lyman County.

I poured him some water from the can we kept in a hole in the ground back of the shack for coolness. He took a swallow and set it down. "Good Lord, how can anyone drink that!" he exclaimed.

"We get used to it," I told him. "And we'll have a better water supply in time. It will rain—it's bound to rain, sooner or later."

He looked out at the blazing sky, the baked earth, a snake slithering from the path back into the dry grass which rustled as it moved. "So this is the land you want to save," he exclaimed. "The incredible thing is that people have managed to stay on it at all!"

"They will stay," I assured him. "Remember that these builders have had nothing to work with, no direction, no system or leadership. What would business men accomplish in such an undertaking under the circumstances? If they had experienced leaders—men like you—"

"In other words," he smiled, "laying up riches where moth and rust do corrupt." He walked to the door and stood, hands in pockets, looking out over the plains. Then he turned to face me.

"My dear girl, I might not be worth a hoot at the job."

"Oh, you would! You would! And if the settlers never repaid you, think what a land king you would become," I laughed.

"No, I don't want the land that way. I want to see the settlers succeed, try to keep them from being squeezed out."

He mopped his face, picked up the glass of water and after a glance at it set it down untouched. "Now, I've been thinking of this western development for some time. It's going to open up new business in almost every field. Aside from all that, it is worth while. I've kept track of you and your Brulé. If one gets his money back here it is all he can expect. How much would be needed to help these settlers hold on—a little grubstake, some future operating money? I like this fallowing idea."

He talked about second mortgages, collateral on personal property, appointment of local agents, etc. He did not want the source of this borrowing power to become known as yet.

It was he who brought me back to my personal predicament when, ready to leave, he expressed his desire to help me, asking if I would accept a check—"For you and your sister to carry on." But I refused. I had appealed to him for the country, not for myself. But his offer mortified me, made me conscious of my shabby appearance, the coarse, ill-fitting clothes, the effects of the fire still visible in rough and smoke-stained skin, the splotches of new skin on my lips, the face pink and tender. Altogether, the surroundings and I must have made a drab spectacle.

Holding out his hand to say good-by, Halbert Donovan saw my shrinking embarrassment. Suddenly he put his arm around my shoulders, drew me to him, brushed back the singed hair and pressed his lips to my forehead; turned my small, blackened hand, palm upward, looking at it.

"I'll help you all I can," he said. "Just keep your Utopian dreams."

So it happened that, before famine could touch these people who had already struggled through drought and blizzard and despair, they found help in sight. Halbert Donovan put up $50,000 as a start, to be dealt out for emergency on land, livestock, etc. Heretofore loans had been made on land only. Now the reliability of the borrower himself was often taken into account as collateral. It was enough that we knew the borrower was honest, that he was doing his best to conquer the land and to make it yield. We gambled on futures then, as we had done before. That it was eastern capital, handled through a system of exchange and agencies, was all that those who borrowed knew or cared.

And each day we scanned the heavens for signs of rain. We searched for a cloud like a starving man for bread. The settlers went stalking about with necks craned, heads thrown back, eyes fixed on the sky. And the cartoonist from Milwaukee took to looking for a cloud with a field glass. A cloud no bigger than a man's hand would raise the hopes of the whole reservation. But in vain we searched the metallic blue of the sky.

With spectacular ceremonial and regalia the Indians staged their "rain dance." The missionaries had long opposed this form of expression by the Indians, and their objections led to a government ban which was finally modified to permit some sort of ritual.

These symbolic dances were not mere ceremonials for the Plains Indians; they were their one means of expressing their emotions en masse rhythmically, of maintaining their sense of tribal unity.

The first part of the ceremony was secret and lasted for several days. After that the public ceremony began. Painted according to ritual, they danced in a line from east to west and back again, whistling as they danced, every gesture having its symbolic meaning. The whistle symbolized to them the call of the Thunderbird.

Pioneers belong to the past, people are prone to say; savage customs belong to the past. But it was in the twentieth century that primitive men, their bodies streaked with black paint, fasted and danced, overcoming an enemy as they danced, compelling the Thunderbird to release the rain. And on the Strip men and women prayed as fervently to their own God, each in his own way.

That night, something breaking the dead stillness woke me. A soft, slow tapping on the roof of the shack, like ghostly fingers. It increased in tempo as though birds, in this land without trees, were pecking at the roof; it grew to a regular drumming sound. I lay for a few moments, listening, wondering. Then I leaped out of bed, ran to the door and stepped outside.

Rain! Rain! Rain!

"Ida Mary," I called, "get up! It's raining!"

She was out of bed in a moment as though someone had shouted "fire."

In nightdress, bare feet, we ran out on the prairie, reached up our hands to the soft, cool, soothing drops which fell slowly as though hesitating whether to fall or not. And then it poured. The grass was wet beneath our feet.

We lifted our heads, opened our lips and drank in the cool, fresh drops. I lay down on the cool blanket of earth, absorbing its reviving moisture into my body, feeling the rain pattering on my flesh.

Over the prairie dim lights flickered through the rain. Men and women rushed out to hail its coming—and to put tubs and buckets under the roofs. No drop of this miracle must be wasted. In their joy and relief, some of the homesteaders, unable to sleep, hitched up and drove across the plains to rejoice with their friends.

After that eternity of waiting it rained and rained, until the earth all about was green and fresh. Native hay came out green, and late-planted seed burst out of the ground. Some of the late crops matured. There was water in the dams! The thirsty land drank deep of the healing rains.

The air grew fresh and cool, haggard faces were alight with hope. The Lower Brulé became a different place, where once again people planned for the future, unafraid to look ahead.

With the mail bag, the salvaged type, and Margaret's few sticks of furniture which she wrote to us to take, we moved back to the homestead, to the site of Ammons.

The settlers had the building up. This time it was a little square-roofed house made of drop siding (no more tar paper). A thin, wallboard partition running halfway to the ceiling divided the small living quarters from the print shop.

The McClure *Press* had died the natural death of the proof sheet, and the proof king was submerged in the cause of prohibition. Later he was appointed federal prohibition agent for the state of South Dakota. He gave us most of the McClure *Press* equipment. So I got that hand press, after all. What few proofs were yet to be made in that section were thrown to *The Wand*. With the current proof money coming in we bought the additional supplies necessary to run the paper.

I sent a telegram to Halbert Donovan: "Rain. Pastures coming out green. Dwarfed grain can make feed in the straw. My flax making part crop. Dams full of water. Fall fallowing begun." In hilarious mood I signed it "Utopia."

Delivered the twenty-five miles in the middle of the night, special messenger service prepaid, came the answer: "Atta girl. Am increasing the stakes."

He did. Halbert Donovan's company interested other financial concerns in making loans, "to deal out through competent appraisement."

So the Brulé won through, as pioneers before them had done, as other pioneers in other regions were doing, as ragged, poverty-stricken, gallant an army as ever marched to the colors.

185

XVII. NEW TRAILS

Ida Mary and Imbert were going to be married. At last Ida Mary was sure, and there was no need of waiting any longer. So she went back to St. Louis for the first time, and two weeks later the wedding took place.

When they returned as bride and groom, the settlers came from every direction, accompanied by all the cow and sheep bells, tin cans and old horns on the Strip for a big charivari. They came bringing baskets of food for the supper and any little article or ornament they could find at home for a wedding present, singing as they came, "Lucky Numbers Are We," and "We Won't Go Home Till Morning."

Imbert took over the Cedar Fork ranch and store—that little trade center outside the reservation gate where a disheveled group of land-seekers had faced a new dawn rising upon the Strip. And Ida Mary, who so loved the land, came at last to make it her permanent home. Steady, practical and resourceful—it was such women the West needed.

The sturdily built log house was a real home, no tar-paper shack—rustic, we would call it now—with four rooms and a porch. There were honest-to-goodness beds, carpets and linoleum on the kitchen floor! Ida Mary was so proud of the linoleum that she wiped it up with skim milk to make it shine. There was a milk cow and conse-quently homemade butter and cottage cheese—all the makeshift discomforts of homesteading replaced by the solid and enduring quali-ties of home.

Peace, home, happiness—for Ida Mary.

And Ma Wagor's problems were solved, too. It appeared that her first husband had left her more than the an-tik brooch of which she was so proud. He had left her a son who had grown to be a stalwart, good-looking young man, who worked with a construction company out in western Nebraska. Learning of the Wagors' misfortune, he came, started another store at Ammons for his mother, and helped her to run it for a while.

All around Ammons the fields lay freshly turned, fallowing for next year's crop. Our field of flax had been cut for what little it would make, and the ground plowed over to soak up the winter's moisture. With the turning of the ground for another season, a page in my own life was turning. "What am I going to do, now that I've come in under the wire?" I wondered.

And then I proved up and got my patent. I borrowed a thousand dollars on it to pay off the government and the balance due our finan-cial backers, who had gambled on us without security. But I did not borrow the money through the Halbert Donovan Company. The loan had been promised me by the banks many months before. We had bor-rowed on the first homestead to get the second, borrowed to the limit on the second to pay for the privilege of helping to run the reservation. We now had both farms mortgaged to the hilt. But the hay alone would pay the interest and taxes. Land would increase in value.

I was alone at the shack now with the newspaper still to get out. Riding across the plains toward the claim one afternoon, I heard the swift, staccato clicking of type as it fell rapidly in the stick. The metal-lic sound carried across the prairie as I neared the shop. As I walked in

I saw, perched on the high stool in front of the type case, a little hoy-denish figure with flying hair—Myrtle Coombs, the hammer-and-tongs printer. "This don't look right to me," she remarked, reading her stick as I came in, "but a good printer follows copy even if it flies out of the window."

Myrtle had come back on vacation to see how her homestead was progressing. Seeing that I needed help, she unrolled a newspaper bundle and hung her "extra" dress and nightgown on a nail, laid a comb and a toothbrush on the dry-goods-box dressing table, and for two weeks she "threw" out the paper with a bang.

About this time the régime of our government was changing. Out of the West, from which we had had only sheep and cattle, there were coming men destined to be leaders in the affairs of the country. As men had risen from the ranks to guide the destinies of the Colonies, so men appeared from the West to shape this new America.

They came from a world where land was king. It was a boundless territory. A large section of it, which was once marked on the map as the Great American Desert, had been left untouched, a dead possession and a problem to the government, who did not know what use to make of it until the homesteaders pushed west.

In the past two or three years, 200,000 homesteaders had taken up claims, filing on more than 40,000,000 acres, making a solid coverage of 70,000 square miles. Those settlers and their families constituted a million people. Ahead of this tidal wave, in the steady stream of im-migration, thousands of other settlers had moved west. Now there were several million people who must subsist on the raw lands. They, with others who had followed the homesteaders, were dependent upon their success or failure to make the western prairie produce.

It had to produce! The West was the nation's reserve of natural resources. The soil was to produce cereal gold, huge fields of wheat, bread for a new people—bread, at last, for a world at war.

So the Public Lands question was of first importance. There must be new land laws and other measures enacted for these people. It was a gigantic task set for the men from out the West to perform. But already they had begun to wield an influence on the affairs of the nation.

One heard of a man from Utah with the name of Smoot, who came from a class of solid builders. He was bound to be heard more of in the future, people said; and there appeared in Congress a man whose indomitable force soon became recognized as something to contend with—a man from Idaho named William E. Borah. Two other west-erners had already become statesmen of note. They had sprung from the sagebrush country. Senator Francis E. Warren, and Congressman Frank W. Mondell—both of Wyoming.

Senator Warren devoted a lifetime to the interests of the West. Congressman Mondell, as Speaker of the House and chairman of the Public Lands Committee, was an influence for the homestead country; and from our own state, progressive, fearless, was Senator Peter Norbeck.

The frontier is big, but news travels over it in devious ways, and the work of *The Wand* and of Ida Mary and me began to be known in Washington. My editorial fight for the settlers attracted the attention of these officials from the West. From several of them we received messages, commending our efforts and offering assistance in any feasible way. I also received communications from Senator Warren and Congressman Mondell, commenting upon my comprehension of the homestead issue. I was asked to submit the problems of my people, and in return I sought information from them.

Small things, those frontier newspapers, but *The Wand* had achieved what Ida Mary and I had hoped of it, it had been the voice of the people, a voice heard across the prairie, across the Land of the Burnt Thigh, across the continent to the doors of Congress itself. Its protests, its recommendations were weighed at last by the men best able to help the men and women on the Strip. And the little outlaw printer, to her overwhelming surprise, was being recognized not only on the Strip but beyond it, as an authority on the homesteading project and a champion of the homesteaders.

It was back on the lookout of the outlaw printer and the outlaw horse thieves, that I got another letter from Senator Warren, asking what my plans were for the future and whether I had thought of carrying my work farther on, work where "the harvest was great and the laborers few," he said. Should I decide to go on into new fields, I could depend upon his support. He would recommend my newspaper as an official one; there would be many opportunities, probably government posts for which my particular knowledge would qualify me.

While I was still undetermined as to what to do after my work on the proof sheet was finished, I was not a career woman, and Senator Warren's suggestions received little serious thought. Ida Mary, I thought, was serving the West in the best way for a woman. Needles and thread and bread dough have done more toward preserving nations than bullets, and the women who made homes on the prairie, working valiantly with the meager tools at their command, did more than any other group in settling the West. It was their efforts which turned tar-paper shacks into livable houses, their determination to provide their children with opportunities which built schools and established communities.

I was content for a while to thrust the thought of the future out of my mind, but I continued to watch with tense interest what was happening to the homestead country. A new land law had been passed which had a strong influence on the agricultural development of the West. It doubled the size of homesteads to 320 acres. This would bring farmers and families for permanent building. It would give them more pasture and plenty of land to carry on the fallowing method. To discourage the prove-up-and-run settler, it required three years, a certain amount of fencing and eighty acres plowed to get a deed. It created a new land splurge. A half-section! To the average homeseeker it was like owning the whole frontier.

This law was called the Mondell Act, and President Theodore Roosevelt proclaimed it "a great opportunity for the poor people—and a long stride in the West's progress." Roosevelt had faith in the future of a Greater America. The programs which he initiated were to accomplish tremendous results in the building of the western lands.

With my bent for delving into the effect of land rulings on the settler, I made inquiry regarding certain provisions of the Mondell Act. With the information came a letter from its author, expressing his belief in the advantages of the act to the homeseeker, and describing what it would do in developing the territory farther west. He talked, too, about my work, and my carrying it into new fields. Wyoming was bound to become a homestead Mecca. And he added: "Your experience in South Dakota could, no doubt, be made of great value in aiding in the development of Wyoming."

A few days after I received Congressman Mondell's letter, C. H. West arrived. Usually placid and genial, he was now wrought up. He came at once to the point of his visit. Under the enlarged homestead law he was extending operations farther west, where he was going to settle large tracts. He wanted me to head bands of homeseekers into this new territory, to help colonize it.

We were entering an era of colonization, of doing things in organized groups, cooperative bodies. To the progress which these movements have made in the United States much is owing to the West, where it was developed through necessity.

Eastern men were forming profit-making corporations to colonize western land. Real estate dealers were organizing colonies. Groups of homeseekers were organizing their own bands. Mr. West had many inquiries from such groups, and he had determined to do his own colonizing. They would want me to go to eastern cities, he said, bring the colonists west, and help locate them satisfactorily.

The locating fees, according to Mr. West, would run into money, and he proposed to give me 50 per cent of the profits. "In addition," he promised, "we will advance you a fair salary and all expenses."

I realized that I must face the future. The proof business on the Strip was almost over. Henceforth the paper, and the post office which had been transferred to me on Ida Mary's marriage, would eke out a bare existence. And, as Ma Wagor complained, the Brulé was becoming so settled "it would be havin' a Ladies Aid before long with the women servin' tea and carryin' callin' cards around." That would be no place for me.

For a long time I sat gazing out of the window over the open spaces. What would this mean to the people whom I was to bring west? It was they, not I nor any other individual, whose future must be weighed. The tidal wave of western immigration would reach its crest in the next two or three years, and break over Wyoming, Montana, Colorado—those states bordering the Great Divide. It was to reach its high peak in 1917, when the United States entered the World War.

I remembered the shaking hands, the faces of the men and women who had lost at the Rosebud Drawing. There was still land for them. Land of their own for tenant farmers, land for the homeless. The Land of a Million Shacks—that was the slogan of the frontier.

"Where is this land?" I asked, finally.

"In Wyoming. Across the Dakota-Nebraska line. Reaching into the Rawhide Country," Mr. West explained.

Rawhide country. Lost Trail. "A short-grass range, but rich," Lone Star had said—"an honest-to-God country, bigger'n all creation."

I turned to Mr. West and faced him squarely. "Has it got water?"

He smiled at the sudden vehemence of the question and was ready for it. "Yes, it has water. The finest in the world." Water clear and cold, he told me, could be obtained at two to three hundred feet on almost any spot. Out on the scattered ranches, in the middle of the range, one found windmills pumping all day long. There would be plenty of water for stock and for irrigating small patches.

"All right," I said, "I'll go."

The cartoonist was going back to Milwaukee. "Being here has done something for me," he said. "Seeing so much effort given ungrudgingly for small results, I think. I'm going back and do something with my art. But it's odd—I don't really want to go back."

191

One by one the prove-up-and-run settlers had left the country, but Huey Dunn, Chris Christopherson and others like them were learning to meet the country on its own terms and conquer it. They were there to stay.

A young man appeared who was willing to run the newspaper, and I turned the post office over to Ma Wagor. Amid the weird beating of tom-toms and the hoo-hoo ah-ah-ahhh of the Indians across the trail, I set up my farewell message in *The Wand*. In gorgeous regalia of beads and quills, paint and eagle feathers, the Indians had come to send the Great Spirit with Paleface-Prints-Paper on to the heap big hunting grounds. It was the time of year when "paint" in all the variegated colors was plentiful, gathered from herbs and flowers, yellow, copper, red. The affair was probably more of an excuse to celebrate than an expression of esteem. The Indians never miss an opportunity to stage a show. When they attend a county fair or other public gathering, they load up children, dogs and worldly goods, and in a long procession they set out, arriving several days before the event and celebrating long after it is all over.

They had come prepared to camp for the night at the print shop, going through special incantations for the occasion, but now they were whooping it up around the campfire. I was dragged into the dance and went careening around with old warriors and young bucks, the squaws laughing at my mistakes.

As a farewell editorial I quoted the epitaph once engraved on a tombstone: "He done his damnedest. Angels could do no more."

The eerie sound of the Indian dance had ceased. The flickering campfires had died down. Only two years and four months since Ida Mary and I had broken a trail to that first little homestead shack. And a chapter of my life was closed.

Beyond, in the dark, slept men and women who had endured hardships and struggles and heavy labor; who had plowed up the virgin soil and set their own roots deep in it. They were here to stay.

In those two years they had built a little empire that would endure. There were roads and fences, schools and thriving towns nearby where they could market their products, and during the World War Presho became the second largest hay-shipping point in the United States, with the government buying trainloads of the fine native hay from the tall grass country of the Brulé.

But my work on the Strip was ended. Big as the venture had seemed to me in the beginning, it was only a fraction of the country waiting to be tamed. And beyond there was Wyoming, "bigger'n all creation."

I was going empty-handed, with no fixed program or goal. After the settlers were on the ground, there would be many obstacles which must be overcome. Down to earth again! Even in the initial colonizing I would have to depend on my own initiative, on my influence with the people, and on my understanding of the homestead project. My experience on the Brulé in getting settlers to work together would be invaluable. The field would be new—but the principles of cooperative effort were always the same.

Upon learning that I was going on with the development work, Senator Warren wrote a letter filled with encouragement and information, and Senator Borah expressed his interest.

Wyoming exemplified all the romance, the color, the drama of the old Wild West. It was noted as a land of cowboys, wild horses, and fearless men. As a commonwealth it was invincible. It was one of the greatest sheep and cattle kingdoms in the world, where stockmen grazed their herds over government domain, lords of all they surveyed.

In the past the big cattle and sheep outfits had brooked no interference. One of the worst stockmen-settler wars ever waged had been fought in Wyoming against an invasion of homesteaders, a war that became so bloody the government had to take a hand, calling out the National Guards to settle it. It was this section of the range country that I was to help fill with sodbreakers.

The force of progress made it safer now, with the government and public sentiment back of the homestead movement. These stockman-settler wars, however, were not yet a thing of the past, and despite the years of western development that followed, they continued to break out every now and then in remote range country. In self-preservation stockmen of various sections were making it difficult for the homesteader, and it was certain that colonies of them would not be welcomed with open arms. I knew all this in a general way, of course, but I had no trepidation over the undertaking. My only qualms were on the score of health. It is a poor trail-breaker who cannot travel with strong people, and that was a drawback I couldn't overcome. All I could do was hope for the best and rely on my ability to catch up if I should have to fall behind. I took a chance on it. I rode to Ida Mary's, and found her rocking and sewing and humming to herself in her new home.

"I'm going to help colonize Wyoming," I told her bluntly.

She let her sewing fall to the floor and sat staring at me, standing bold and defiant in the middle of the floor. But my voice broke and I threw myself across her bed crying. It was my first venture without Ida Mary.

She did not say now, as she had done on other occasions: "How can you help colonize a raw range country? You couldn't manage it." Life had done something to us out here.

I started out from Ida Mary's. Out across the plain I turned and looked back. She was still standing in the doorway, shading her eyes so as to see me longer. We waved and waved, and I left her watching as the distance swallowed me up.

At the shack I found Judge Bartine waiting for me. He observed the traces of tears on my cheeks, but made no comment on them.

"You know," he said, "I'm glad you and your sister stuck through all this."

I hesitated, on the verge of telling him how near I had come to giving up and starting a back-trek.

"When the cattle-rustling gang I convicted burned the courthouse and my office over my head," he went on after a little pause, "I made a narrow escape. I didn't have a penny in the world left with which to fight, and I knew perfectly well that I was in danger of being shot down every time I went out of the door.

"But I had to stay. Men could go through Hades out here for years to get a foothold and raise a herd of cattle and wake up one morning to find it gone. Something had to be done with those cattle thieves."

"It seems to me," I told him, "the stockmen should have paid you awfully well."

"I got my pay," he said quietly, "just as you have done; I got my pay in the doing. So, Edith, I am glad you girls did not run away. I didn't come before because I didn't want to influence you. I wanted to see you do it alone."

When he had gone, I closed the door of the shack behind me. A man was riding up the trail to meet me, bringing two messages. One from the House of Representatives in Washington was signed F. W. Mondell. "I am delighted," it read, "to know of your faith and confidence in the country farther west, particularly the region to which you are going. I trust the settlers whom you are instrumental in bringing into the country will be successful, and I have no doubt that they will, if they are the right sort. I wish you Godspeed and success." The other letter was from Mr. West, who was awaiting me on the road to Wyoming with a group of landseekers.

On top of the ridge I stopped and gazed at the cabin with no sign of life around it, took my last look at the Land of the Burnt Thigh. A wilderness I had found it, a thriving community I left it. But the sun was getting low and I had new trails to break.

I gave Lakota the rein.

Also from Benediction Books ...
Wandering Between Two Worlds: Essays on Faith and Art
Anita Mathias
Benediction Books, 2007
152 pages
ISBN: 0955373700

Available from www.amazon.com, www.amazon.co.uk

In these wide-ranging lyrical essays, Anita Mathias writes, in lush, lovely prose, of her naughty Catholic childhood in Jamshedpur, India; her large, eccentric family in Mangalore, a sea-coast town converted by the Portuguese in the sixteenth century; her rebellion and atheism as a teenager in her Himalayan boarding school, run by German missionary nuns, St. Mary's Convent, Nainital; and her abrupt religious conversion after which she entered Mother Teresa's convent in Calcutta as a novice. Later rich, elegant essays explore the dualities of her life as a writer, mother, and Christian in the United States-- Domesticity and Art, Writing and Prayer, and the experience of being "an alien and stranger" as an immigrant in America, sensing the need for roots.

About the Author

Anita Mathias is the author of *Wandering Between Two Worlds: Essays on Faith and Art.* She has a B.A. and M.A. in English from Somerville College, Oxford University, and an M.A. in Creative Writing from the Ohio State University, USA. Anita won a National Endowment of the Arts fellowship in Creative Nonfiction in 1997. She lives in Oxford, England with her husband, Roy, and her daughters, Zoe and Irene.

Visit Anita's website
    http://www.anitamathias.com,
and Anita's blog
    http://dreamingbeneaththespires.blogspot.com, (Dreaming Beneath the Spires).

The Church That Had Too Much
Anita Mathias
Benediction Books, 2010
52 pages
ISBN: 9781849026567

Available from www.amazon.com, www.amazon.co.uk

The Church That Had Too Much was very well-intentioned. She
wanted to love God, she wanted to love people, but she was both
hampered by her muchness and the abundance of her possessions, and beset by ambition, power struggles and snobbery.
Read about the surprising way The Church That Had Too Much
began to resolve her problems in this deceptively simple and en-
chanting fable.

About the Author

Anita Mathias is the author of *Wandering Between Two Worlds:
Essays on Faith and Art.* She has a B.A. and M.A. in English
from Somerville College, Oxford University, and an M.A. in
Creative Writing from the Ohio State University, USA. Anita
won a National Endowment of the Arts fellowship in Creative
Nonfiction in 1997. She lives in Oxford, England with her husband, Roy, and her daughters, Zoe and Irene.

Visit Anita's website
 http://www.anitamathias.com,
and Anita's blog
 http://dreamingbeneaththespires.blogspot.com (Dreaming Beneath the Spires).